The Deadly Night of Octobe...
...Peshtigo Fire
By Charles River Editors

Harper's Weekly illustration of the Great Chicago Fire

About Charles River Editors

Charles River Editors provides superior editing and original writing services across the digital publishing industry, with the expertise to create digital content for publishers across a vast range of subject matter. In addition to providing original digital content for third party publishers, we also republish civilization's greatest literary works, bringing them to new generations of readers via ebooks.

Sign up here to receive updates about free books as we publish them, and visit Our Kindle Author Page to browse today's free promotions and our most recently published Kindle titles.

Introduction

Picture of the ruins at Dearborn and Monroe

The Great Chicago Fire of 1871

"The fire was barely fifteen minutes old. What followed was a series of fatal errors that set the fire free and doomed the city to a fiery death." – Jim Murphy, *The Great Fire*

It had taken about 40 years for Chicago to grow from a small settlement of about 300 people into a thriving metropolis with a population of 300,000, but in just two days in 1871, much of that progress was burned to the ground. In arguably the most famous fire in American history, a blaze in the southwestern section of Chicago began to burn out of control on the night of October 8, 1871. Thanks to *The Chicago Tribune*, the fire has been apocryphally credited to a cow kicking over a lantern in Mrs. Catherine O'Leary's barn, and though that was not true, the rumor dogged Mrs. O'Leary to the grave.

Of course, the cause of the fire didn't matter terribly much to the people who lost their lives or their property in the blaze. Thanks to dry conditions, wind, and wooden buildings, firefighters were never actually able to stop the fire, which burned itself out only after it spent nearly two whole days incinerating several square miles of Chicago. By the time rain mercifully helped to put the fire out, the Great Chicago Fire had already killed an estimated 300 people, destroyed an estimated 17,500 buildings, and left nearly 100,000 people (1/3 of the population) homeless.

Several other theories have developed as an explanation for the fire. Most of them center on people around Mrs. O'Leary's barn, but other have gone so far as to blame a meteor shower as the culprit that started fires across the Midwest that same night. As proof, they note that the country's worst forest fire in history took place around the same time in the logging town of Peshtigo in northeastern Wisconsin, a fire that killed thousands.

Mrs. O'Leary and her barn remain a part of lore, but it also speaks to Chicago's ability to rebuild that it's almost impossible to envision a farm in downtown Chicago today. Chicago suffered a wide swath of destruction, but it had rebuilt itself within 20 years in order to host the World's Fair, evidence that it was back and bigger and better than ever. Along with that, Chicago has maintained its status as the region's biggest city and one of the most important in America.

The Deadly Night of October 8, 1871 chronicles one of the largest natural disasters of the 19th century in America. Along with pictures of important people, places, and events, you will learn about the Great Chicago Fire of 1871 like never before, in no time at all.

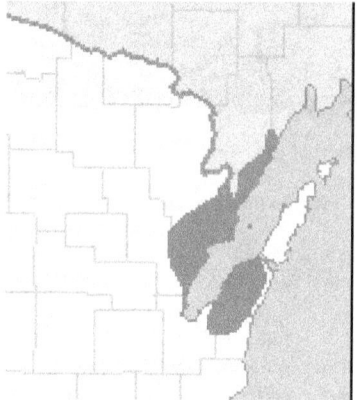

The extent of the fire damage in Wisconsin and the Upper Peninsula of Michigan

The Peshtigo Fire of 1871

"Why is this story not known? You see endless stories about Johnstown. What happened at Peshtigo makes Johnstown look like a birdbath." – Bill Lutz, co-author of *Firestorm at Peshtigo*

"The air burned hotter than a crematorium and the fire traveled at 90 mph. I read an account of a Civil War veteran who had been through some of the worst battles of the war. He described the sound - the roar - during the fire as 100 times greater than any artillery bombardment." – Bill Lutz

Due to the publicity generated by a fire that reduced most of a major American city to ash, the Peshtigo Fire of 1871 might fairly be called America's forgotten disaster. Overshadowed by the much better covered and publicized Great Chicago Fire that occurred on the same evening, the fire that started in the Wisconsin logging town of Peshtigo generated a firestorm unlike anything in American history. In addition to destroying a wide swath of land, it killed at least 1,500 people and possibly as many as 2,500, several times more than the number of casualties in Chicago. While people marveled at the fact that the Great Chicago Fire managed to jump a river, the Peshtigo fire was so intense that it was able to jump several miles across Green Bay. While wondering aloud about the way in which the Peshtigo fire has been overlooked, Bill Lutz noted, "Fires are normally very fascinating to people, but people seem resistant to Peshtigo. Maybe Peshtigo is on such a large scale that people can't comprehend it."

Ironically, while Peshtigo is widely forgotten, the fire there is often cited as proof that the Great Chicago Fire was caused by natural phenomena, such as a comet or meteor shower. Those advocating such a theory think it's too coincidental that such disastrous fires were sparked in the same region on the same night, and they point to other fires across the Midwest. Of course, as with the Great Chicago Fire, contemporaries of the Peshtigo fire faulted human error and didn't necessarily link the two fires, if only because fires were a common problem in both Peshtigo and Chicago during the 19th century.

The Deadly Night of October 8, 1871 chronicles the story America's deadliest fire. Along with pictures of important people, places, and events, you will learn about the Peshtigo fire like never before, in no time at all.

The Deadly Night of October 8, 1871: The Great Chicago Fire and the Peshtigo Fire

About Charles River Editors

Introduction

The Great Chicago Fire

   Chapter 1: The O'Leary Legend

   Chapter 2: Wood, Wind and Fire

   Chapter 3: The Circumstances Were Terrifying

   Chapter 4: Across the River

   Chapter 5: The Water Runs Out

   Chapter 6: Evacuation

   Chapter 7: Order

   Chapter 8: Survival

   Chapter 9: Protection

   Chapter 10: Rebuilding

The Peshtigo Fire

   Chapter 1: A Source of Prosperity

   Chapter 2: Two Different Impressions

   Chapter 3: The Crimson Reflection, the Muttered Thunder

   Chapter 4: Seek the River at Once

   Chapter 5: Near the River

   Chapter 6: Appalling Dangers

   Chapter 7: Nothing But Flames

   Chapter 8: An End to All Things

   Chapter 9: Survivors After a Battle

   Chapter 10: Nothing Whatever Remained

   Chapter 11: Wandering Among the Ruins

Bibliography

The Great Chicago Fire

Chapter 1: The O'Leary Legend

A map showing the section of Chicago that burned in the fire, with Mrs. O'Leary's barn marked by a red dot in the southwestern part of the damaged section.

"I was in bed myself and my husband and five children when this fire commenced. I was the owner of them five cows that was burnt, and the horse wagon and harness. I had two tons of coal and two tons of hay. I had everything that I wanted in for the winter. I could not save five cents worth of anything out of the barn. Only that Mr. Sullivan got out a little calf. The calf was worth eleven dollars on Saturday morning. Saturday morning I refused even eleven dollars for the calf, and it was sold afterwards for eight dollars. I didn't save five cents out of the fire. I could not tell anything of the fire only that two men came by the door. I guess it was my husband got outside the door and he ran back to the bedroom and said 'Kate the barn is afire.' I ran out and the whole barn was on fire. Well I went out to the barn and upon my word I could not tell anyone about the fire. I got just the way I could not tell anything about the fire." - Catherine O'Leary

Although people who have only passing familiarity with the Great Chicago Fire often know the legend about Mrs. O'Leary's cow, little is actually known for certain about how the fire began. It was pretty clear that the fire began a short while after 9:00 p.m. on Sunday evening, October 8, 1871, but even before the last flame had died down, a colorful legend had grown up around the cause of the fire. While there were many different versions of the original story, the gist of it was that Kate O'Leary went out after dark to care for or check on her cows, and for some reason, she left the kerosene lantern she was carrying with her in the barn. Then, after she went back into the house, one of her cows kicked it over, spilling the oil and igniting the hay.

SUPPOSED CAUSE OF THE CHICAGO FIRE. MRS. O'LEARY AND HER COW.

A Harper's Magazine **illustration depicting O'Leary and her cow**

Although the legend sounds fanciful today, there were several reasons why the story seemed plausible to investigators. First, according to the board who reviewed the evidence, "the fire originated in a two-story barn in the rear of No. 137 DeKoven Street, the premises being owned by Patrick O'Leary. The fire was first discovered by a drayman by the name of Daniel [Dennis] Sullivan, who saw it while sitting on the sidewalk on the south side of DeKoven Street, and nearly opposite O'Leary's premises. He fixes the time at not more than twenty or twenty-five minutes past nine o'clock when he first noticed the flames coming out of the barn. There is no proof that any person had been in the barn after nightfall that evening. Whether it originated from a spark blown from a chimney on that windy night, or was set on fire by human agency, we are unable to determine. Mr. O'Leary and all his family prove to have been in bed and asleep at the time. There was a small party in the front part of O'Leary's house, which was occupied by Mr. McLaughlin and wife. But we fail to find any evidence that anybody from McLaughlin's part of the house went near the barn that night." Furthermore, the O'Leary's did keep cows in that barn, and the cows would have needed care on the farm.

The O'Leary house at No. 137 DeKoven Street

However, except in the case of a cow giving birth, there would be no reason for anyone to have gone to the barn at night. Milking was done in the morning and the evening, but always during daylight hours, meaning there would have been no reason for Mrs. O'Leary to leave a lighted lamp in the barn. Not only would it potentially start a fire, it would also waste oil, which the O'Leary's could not afford to waste.

Of course, the most damning evidence refuting the story came from the man who originally published it. 22 years later, Michael Ahern publically admitted that he had added the story to his original article on the fire to lend some local color to the event.

If indeed the fire was started as a result of someone or something on the O'Leary farm, there were better suspects than Mrs. O'Leary or her cows. According to O'Leary's testimony before the board investigating the fire, there was quite a party going on in another part of the house that night. The family had rented two front rooms to the McLaughlin's, who were the ones throwing the party, and while O'Leary maintained that she was not in attendance, she claimed she could hear what was going on. This led to speculation on some people's parts that there was also gambling going on in the barn, which would at least would present a plausible reason for there being a lit lamp out there. Someone could have knocked it over, especially if there was alcohol involved, and then chose to run rather than try to put it out. In fact, according to an article published decades later, Louis Cohn, then a well-respected world traveler, was honored by Northwestern University's Medill School of Journalism for his large contribution to the college, Cohn maintained for years that he was responsible for the fire: "Mr. Cohn had an interesting connection with the origin of the Great Chicago Fire. He steadfastly maintained that the traditional story of the cause of the fire -- Mrs. O'Leary's cow that kicked over a lantern -- was untrue. He asserted that he and Mrs. O'Leary's son, in the company of several other boys, were shooting dice in the hayloft . . . by the light of a lantern, when one of the boys accidently overturned the lantern, thus setting the barn afire. Mr. Cohn never denied that when the other boys fled, he stopped long enough to scoop up the money."

While O'Leary and Louie Cohn have stories that offer a down-to-earth explanation for the fire, Ignatius Donnelly had a much more heavenly explanation. He speculated that the fire was caused by a meteor shower created when Biela's comet lost its tail. In defending his theory, he pointed accurately to other fires that broke out at that time around the Midwest: "At that hour, half past nine o'clock in the evening, at apparently the same moment, at points hundreds of miles apart, in three different States, Wisconsin, Michigan, and Illinois, fires of the most peculiar and devastating kind broke out, so far as we know, by spontaneous combustion. In Wisconsin, on its eastern borders, in a heavily timbered country, near Lake Michigan, a region embracing four hundred square miles, extending north from Brown County, and containing Peshtigo, Manistee, Holland, and numerous villages on the shores of Green Bay, was swept bare by an absolute whirlwind of flame. There were seven hundred and fifty people killed outright, besides great numbers of the wounded, maimed, and burned, who died afterward. More than three million dollars' worth of property was destroyed." While the meteorite explanation still has a number of defenders, it has never gained wide spread popularity in the scientific community.

Chapter 2: Wood, Wind and Fire

"This season has been the dryest in the West for years. We hadn't had a drop of rain for months, and there had been but one cloudy day during the month of September. The result was that the dust was almost intolerable, the ground became parched, and the houses were as dry as tinder. Besides a furious wind from the southwest had been blowing steadily all day Sunday, one of the most violent winds I ever saw in a clear day." - William Gallagher

Though the fire ultimately spread out of control, the fire department reported that it was able to respond immediately to the reported blaze: "The first information received by the Fire Department came from the alarm struck in the fire-alarm office at 9:30. The alarm sounded Box No. 342, at the corner of Canalport Avenue and Halsted Street, a point in the direction of the fire, but a mile beyond it. There was no signal given by any box to the central office, but the box was given by Mathias Schaffer, from the Court house cupola, he being the night watchman on duty at the time, and having sighted the fire. There was no signal given from anybody until after the Fire Department had arrived and turned in the second and third alarms. If any person set the fire, either by accident or design, he was careful not to give the alarm. The nearest engine-house was six blocks from the fire; the next nearest one was nine blocks away. The nearest hose-house was located eleven blocks from the fire, and, at this hose-house, the watchman had seen the fire before the alarm was given from the Court House, and the company were on their way to the fire before the box was struck."

The Courthouse after the fire

The problem was that Chicago was the scene of a perfect storm of circumstances that conspired together to spread the fire. First, there were the houses themselves; at that time, wood was still the favorite choice of building material in the Midwest, and more than half of all the structures in Chicago were made of wood. Furthermore, even the city's sidewalks were made of wood, providing excellent paths for the fire to travel on from one building to the next. Writing a month after the catastrophe, noted architect Frederick Olmsted blamed the way in which the city constructed its large building for helping spread the fire: "Some ostensibly stone fronts had huge overhanging wooden or sheet-metal cornices fastened directly to their roof timbers, with wooden parapets above them. Flat roofs covered with tarred felt and pebbles were common. In most cases, I am told by observers, the fire entered the great buildings by their roof timbers, even common sheet-metal seeming to offer but slight and very temporary protection to the wood on which it rested. Plain brick walls or walls of brick with solid stone quoins and window-dressings evidently resisted the fire much better than stone-faced walls with a thin backing of brick."

Frederick Olmsted

That said, if the weather and season had been normal, it is unlikely that the fire would have gotten out of hand. Unfortunately, Chicago and much of the Midwest had suffered a severe drought during the summer of 1871, as meteorologists recorded just one inch of rainfall between July 4 and the day of the fire. The effects were still being felt, even in the cities. People had gone from making random comments about the heat to asking each other how long it'd been since it rained. As the drought continued, people started remarking about how important it was to be careful with fire. Public service announcements followed that, with everyone warned to be on the lookout for fire.

Of course, it was impossible during the 19th century to avoid using fire altogether. After all, every morning began with building a fire in the cook stove to make breakfast, and every evening ended around a kerosene lamp or, in wealthier homes, gaslight. In between, fire was used to keep homes warm and even to power steam engines in factories. At the same time, since most people lived with fire all the time, they were more comfortable with it, which could lead to additional care or to carelessness. In October 1871, it may have been the latter.

In addition to the drought, there was also the matter of wind that night. One fireman later wrote, "When they arrived there from three to five buildings were fiercely burning. The fire must have been burning from ten to fifteen minutes; and with the wind then blowing strongly from the southwest, and carrying the fire from building to building in a neighborhood composed wholly of dry wooden buildings, with wood shavings piled in every barn and under every house, the fire had got under too great headway for the engines called out by the first alarm to be able to subdue it…Marshal Williams immediately ordered the second, and, soon afterward, the third, alarm to be turned in, but … before this could be accomplished, the strong wind had scattered the fire into the many buildings, all as dry as tinder, and spread it over so large an area that the whole Department … were unable to cut it off or prevent the wind, which soon became a gale, from carrying burning shingles and brands over their heads, and setting on fire buildings far away from the main fire."

Finally, there was the matter of how close the buildings were to each other. In 1871, Chicago was in the middle of a huge growth spurt as people flocked to the city looking for work. Many were veterans of the Civil War who had growing families and needed places to live. Unable to afford much land, they built rambling houses on small lots, making the best use of the space possible. As a result, many neighboring rooftops nearly touched each other, making it easy for fires to leap from one building to the next.

Chapter 3: The Circumstances Were Terrifying

"[I]t was Sunday night after evening church that the sky became red again in the southwest, and rumors of a big fire in that direction were circulated. Soon it was heard that the Fire Department had lost control of it; and as there had been a drought, and as a large part of Chicago consisted of wooden buildings, there was a good deal of alarm felt. The four younger children were in bed, Lida and I in one room, and Dora and Emily in another. The rest of the family was in the library with neighbors who were watching the fire with them from the windows…The sky kept getting red and redder; the wind, already high, was increasing with the heat, and huge burning cinders were settling in every direction…Mother became very worried about Father, because it was after midnight; the fire was sweeping nearer; refugees loaded with goods were going north by our house; and altogether the circumstances were terrifying." - Ada Rumsey

In the years leading up to the fire, the city had grown to the point of averaging two fires a day somewhere in the area, but this was not overwhelming since the fire department was well-equipped with 17 horse drawn engines and staffed with more than 180 men. However, the frequency with which they were able to put out fires led to a certain complacency on the part of some of the firefighters, including the two Otis brothers. Their sister, Jennie, later recalled, "The room I occupied faced the west, being the back of the house. My two older brothers having the front room on the same floor. I had only been asleep a short while when I was awakened by the fire bells, which we had in those days, and the clanging of engines. My room windows had no shades, but inside blinds. As they were open, I saw the first of this west side fire. The wind was very strong from the south-west, blowing the flames toward the lake and the north side. It grew larger and larger, and after an hour I decided to go and call my brothers. As they had been to the fire the night before and were tired, they did not seem interested, and I returned to my room again, watched the fire leaping and spreading at a terrific rate. In a short while I decided to go again to my brothers' room; this time I was told to go back to bed and forget it."

Tragically, the fire her brothers had fought the night before had also been worked on by many other members of the Chicago Fire Department, leaving them exhausted. This was an important fact to keep in mind when examining any mistakes that may have been made, especially since many members of the department were called upon to give as much as 48 hours of uninterrupted service to very strenuous work, all while being tasked with attempting to use good judgment in making decisions on a scale they had never experienced before.

Though the men were able to put out the initial fire at the O'Leary barn, it had spread to other buildings before they were done. The firemen then changed their tactics and swung their engines around in an effort to stop the fire from the north, but by the time they got to their new location, sometime around 10:30, the fire was already ahead of them and forced them to fall back and move north again. By this time, their efforts were being hampered by the crowds of people flying into the streets and fleeing from the fire with whatever they could carry. Clarence Burley encountered these crowds himself and later recalled, "As I reached Kinzie Street I saw that flames were leaping across Clark Street some blocks South of the river. Many people were coming across the bridge. I thought the tunnel would be a better way to get to the other side. I found the foot passage of the tunnel full of people, with bundles and trunks of belongings, and just as I reached the entrance the gas went out."

Meanwhile, most of the citizens and visitors to Chicago continued to go about their business as if nothing was amiss. The latter group included Alfred Hebard and his family, who were only passing through Chicago and were spending the night at the Palmer Hotel. The building had been open to the public for less than two weeks, and Mrs. Hebard later described the scene: "Returning from an evening [church] service, we were told that another fire had broken out in the western part of the city and was progressing rapidly. We immediately took the elevator to the upper story of the Palmer, saw the fire, but, deciding that it would not cross the river, descended to our rooms in the second story to prepare for sleep. Husband and daughter soon retired; I remained up to prepare for the morrow's journey, and thus gain a little time for shopping before the departure of the train at 11 A.M. Feeling somewhat uneasy, I frequently opened the blinds, and each time found the light in the streets increased until every spire and dome seemed illuminated. I aroused my husband, asking him to go out and investigate once more, which he did, telling me, on his return, not to be alarmed, as there was no danger in our locality."

A picture of the Palmer House before the fire

By around 11:30 PM, the fire had spread well past DeKoven Street and was approaching the Chicago River. At this point, firefighters could only hope that the river itself was wide enough to stop the blaze from spreading any more, and they were encouraged by the fact that the previous night's fire had been in the same area, so much of what might fuel the current fire was already gone. However, their hopes were soon dashed as the bridges themselves caught fire and sent it across the water to the lumber yards and warehouses on the other side. Sparks and the debris from the fire also blew across the river and began landing on other structures, among them the South Side Gas Works. One witness remembered, "The fire on the West Side was fast burning to a point where it must stop--on the grounds burned over the night previous, when all at once the

South Side caught, near or at the Gas Works. I would have gone over then--had just seen the C & N Freight houses burn--but wanted the gas works to blow up before I went among the high stone buildings of the South Side. In less than half an hour I went over, after the explosion, and the whole portion of the South Side seemed to be on fire--all west of Dearborn. The burning shingle, pieces of lumber, paper roofing and every conceivable thing came rushing down through the air like snow, all was smoke and sparks and the wind would gather them up again building in huge windows for coals."

Chapter 4: Across the River

The Crosby Opera House before the fire

"Half past one Monday morning we were awakened by a loud knocking at the front door we were awake in an instant and dressing ourselves we looked about and saw a perfect shower of sparks flying over our house. I got some water and went out in the yard while my brother went up on the roof we worked for one or two hours at the end of that time we had to give up. We tried to get a wagon but could not so we put two trunks on a wheelbarrow and each of us shouldered a bundle and we marched for the old skating park I leading my goat. We got along very well until the Peshtigo Lumber yard caught on fire then it was all we could do to breathe. Mother caught on fire once but we put it out. At last we heard that there was a little shanty that hadn't burnt down so we marched there but had to leave our trunks and everything else but Charlie and father went back and got one but could not get the other as the sand was blowing in their faces and cut like glass at last a wagon drove up and we all piled in and escaped..." - Justin Butterfield

The loss of the gas plant only made things even more dangerous for those still trying to survive in the fire's path. In large cities like Chicago at the time, most of the larger houses were lit by gas lighting that was pumped to the houses by the station, so when the station was gone, people were forced to resort other sources of light, even while they continued to try to keep their homes from burning By this time, Alfred Hebard and his family had reached the home of their friends the Hubbard's and joined a large number of people taking refuge there. Mrs. Hebard explained, "The fire, meanwhile, was coming nearer, and just as we began in earnest to pack necessary things for removal, the Gasworks were destroyed and candles had to be resorted to. Everyone thought the house might be saved, standing as it did on a corner and disconnected from every other building, but we worked on through the night, preparing for the worst, and running often to the garret to see if the worst was not over. In the early morning men came, tore up carpets to cover the roof, draining both cisterns to keep the carpets wet, hoping if possible to stop the fire at that corner. Oh, how they worked! The thoughtful family provided refreshments as long as it was possible, and when all supplies were exhausted the men labored on, panting and parched with thirst, drinking the very dregs of the cistern water from tubs in the kitchen as they passed through. All said, 'This house will not burn!' but they might as well have tried to quench Vesuvius. The heat increased. A wooden block nearby flashed into flame, and at 11 A.M. the cornice was blazing, and we were obliged to go out through the alley to escape the heat and cinders; but where to go we could not tell."

Once the fire jumped the river, it was obvious that the fire department would not be able to stop it. Furthermore, the wind itself had become so hot as a result of the flames that it was fanning, and the heat generated by the wind was enough to set fire to buildings before the fire ever reached them. Naturally, more and more people began to panic and evacuate their homes, as Ada Rumsey later recalled: "We hoped the river would prove a barrier to the flames, but this was not to be. Huge burning brands were carried by the wind, starting new fires in places…Christian [a servant to the family] had harnessed our two little black ponies to a phaeton belonging to my older sisters, and into this was put a clothes basket filled with silver and linen with some other things gathered up by Mother and Sister Meme. Also in the carriage were put the portraits of Father, Mother, and Grandfather Turner, and one or two other paintings…By this time houses were burning about us and our own house was on fire. The streets were filled with vehicles loaded with household goods, and with people staggering under big loads. Mother had waited for Father but was feeling that it would not be safe for us to stay much longer, when he appeared begrimed and tired. In his hand he carried a tin box of papers which he gave to Christian, who was just about to drive from the house with his load. Father said he did not know what was in the box, but it represented all the wealth he then possessed. So Christian drove off into the night with all that was left to us."

Sometime between midnight and 2:00 a.m., the mayor of the city, Roswell B. Mason, decided it was time to send to other communities for help, a fact underscored by the fact that the courthouse in which he had been working had been evacuated and caught fire. When the cupola containing the town's great bell collapsed at 2:20, the sound was so loud that it was heard a mile away, but by then, people across the city had to worry about the fact that much of the city was being consumed. William Gallagher noted, "At half-past two I was awakened by a tremendous knocking at my door, and on opening it I found one of my companions of the night before, who told me that Chicago was all on fire, that the Court House was gone, that all the business part of the city was in flames, and that he and his 'chum' were going down town. I dressed hastily, climbed to the roof, and saw a sight such as I never expect to see again, and which few men have had the privilege of witnessing...There was a strip of fire between two and three miles long, and a mile wide, hurried along by a wind that I have never seen excelled except by our September gale, sweeping through the business part of this city. We were situated where we could take in the whole at a sight, and such a view such a magnificent sight!"

Mayor Mason

Part of what drove the fire on through the night was "fire whirl," a meteorological situation that often occurs when large fires sweep across congested areas. As the overheated air rose into the sky, it came in contact with cooler air, which in turn caused it to cool suddenly and fall to earth. This created a sort of burning tornado that not only lit things on fire but also threw burning debris toward other areas, thereby starting new fires. When some of the debris kicked up by the fire whirl landed in a railroad car full of kerosene, it spread the blaze further and helped the fire jump the river again so that it began burning the north side of the city. According to Julia Lemos, "[A]bout five o'clock in the morning was woke up by a rumbling noise, so as I was awake I got up and threw open the shutters, I thought I was dreaming, the whole street was crowded with people, with hats and shawls on, a neighbor who stood in front of our house called to me, and said Mrs. Lemos, are you just getting up? I said yes, what is the matter? The sky was reflecting fire, she said the city has been burning all night, and the fire is coming to the north side, Well, that startled me, and I ran to the back room and called my father and mother up, I said the city is burning…by that time the fire was advancing on us, I wanted to leave the house, but father said, O, the wind will change. People were running in crowds past our house, I stood with my baby in my arms and the other children beside me, when a woman running past with three children, said to me, Madam, ain't you going to save those children, that started me, I went to Father and said I was going to leave at once…"

Chapter 5: The Water Runs Out

A picture of the ruins that appeared in *The New York Times*

A picture of the ruins on LaSalle St.

The Palmer House after the fire

"As thousands fled to the North Division, the fire pursued them. By 3:30 a.m., the roof collapsed on the Pumping Station at Chicago Avenue, effectively rendering any firefighting efforts hopeless. By noon on Monday the North Division fires had reached North Avenue and then continued the better part of a mile to Fullerton Avenue. Back in the South Division, the luxurious new Palmer House gave way, along with the offices of the Chicago Tribune, whose editors had exhorted the Common Council to raise the level of fire protection or face disaster. Tuesday morning a rain began to fall, and the flames finally died out, leaving Chicago a smoking, steaming ruin." - Bessie Bradwell Helmer

Although the situation was becoming increasingly hopeless, the firefighters continued to fight in an effort to save what they could. One of their main concerns was trying to keep the city's water supply flowing, not only to fight the fires but to ensure people still had water to drink. Unfortunately, the efforts were futile once a burning piece of wood from one building fell onto the roof of the facility and set it on fire. As the roof burned and fell through, pieces of it fell into the machinery and broke it, bringing the pumps to a halt. For the next few weeks, the citizens of the city were wholly dependent on the few older wells still in use around town for water.

Even worse, there was no more water with which to fight the fires. William Carter was among the first to see the damage: "Between one and two in the morning I went home, took Kate and the children to a place of safety, ordered the bedding and other things to be packed--went for teams--a difficult thing to find at that time of the night and then drove with all speed to the water works. My anxiety for the water works was due not more to save the buildings than to save a supply to the people to drink. It was too late, after going around in order to reach a spot of safety nearly five miles, I had to abandon the attempt and turned back almost in despair. The flames were rushing most frantically, leaping from block to block--whole squares vanishing as though they were gossamer."

Without water, the fire department quickly began trying to think of another way to stop the fire, and they decided to try to create some sort of fire break between where the fire was burning at the time and the rest of the city. In order to do this, they would have to take a very large chance by blowing up several buildings that were still standing. According the official report filed after the fire, "The engines had all been working on the West Side; and they could not reel-up six hundred feet of hose each, and cross the river, and get to work soon enough to prevent it spreading, literally, on the wings of the wind. Blowing up buildings in the face of the wind was tried, but without any benefit. The Court House and the Water Works, though a mile apart, were burning at the same time. Gunpowder was used in blowing up buildings, with good effect, the next day, in cutting off the fire at the extreme south end of it, and preventing it backing any further. After the Water Works burned, the firemen could do little good with their engines, except on the banks of the river."

From that point forward, the fire burned with no resistance, constantly perpetuating itself through the spread of ash and sparks. It spread across the city to areas that had not yet been burned, brought by the winds that continued to blow unabated through the night. Cassius Wicker later remembered, "Tops of all the buildings as well as the street were all a blaze. Chamber of Commerce and cupola of the C & N were a blaze, and flying embers and sheets of flame were born against the Skinner house, and falling would break into a thousand pieces, only to be born again into some basement, or further down the street by the perfect hurricane of a wind."

Though they had no water, the firefighters continued to fight on through the night by taking the hoses and pumps to the river and getting as much water from there as they could in order to keep up their battle against the spreading flames. These efforts were complicated by the fact that they had already lost a bunch of their equipment, and there was only so much they could do under those circumstances: "After the Water Works burned, the firemen could do little good with their engines, except on the banks of the river. They had lost seven thousand five hundred feet of hose and one steam fire engine. Two more engines had been in the repair shops…and, after daybreak, only one-half of our hose remained. This would not [allow] an engine conveying water very far from the river. The firemen and their officers were sober, and did all that men could do. They worked heroically to save the property of others, when their own houses were burning and their families fleeing from the flames. A large part of the Department had worked on Saturday night, and Sunday until 3 p.m.--eighteen hours' steady work,--and they were nearly exhausted when this fire commenced; but they responded to the call with alacrity and worked with all their remaining energy."

Chapter 6: Evacuation

Ruins from the interior of St. Paul's Church

The remains of the Lake-Side Publishing Company

"Chicago had a weakness for 'big things,' and liked to think that it was outbuilding New York. It did a great deal of commercial advertising in its house-tops. The faults of construction as well as of art in its great showy buildings must have been numerous. Their walls were thin, and were overweighted with gross and coarse misornamentation." – Frederick Olmsted

People were already terrified before word began to spread that the fire was out of control. However, while there was still water, there was hope that their brave firemen could get the fire under control, and that even if others' houses were burning, their own homes might be spared. Likewise, the Hebard's and the other visitors staying in the Palmer Hotel continued to hope for the best. After all, many had heard that its developer, Potter Palmer, called the hotel "The World's First Fireproof Building," but he was about to being proven terribly wrong. Mrs. Hebard later wrote, "About 11 P.M. I retired, but could not sleep, and it seemed not more than half an hour before there was a rapping at every door, and finally at ours, to which my husband responded very coolly, 'What's wanted?' 'Fire, sir!' was the answer, and the same moment we were on our feet. Our daughter was awakened, toilets soon made, and no time wasted in gathering together bags and shawls ready for departure. By this time my husband, who had stepped out to reconnoiter, returned, saying that everyone was stirring, and that he saw gentlemen dragging their own trunks down the stairs. The clerks at the office assured him there was no immediate danger, but they thought it well enough to be prepared. Then we all went once more to the seventh story, looked in vain for any evidence that the fire was decreasing, returned to our room, picked up our parcels, including the trunk (for no porters were to be found), descended to the office, paid our bill, and sat down to watch and wait. Finally, leaving our daughter in charge of the baggage, I went with my husband into the street, and around to the rear of the building where the fire was distinctly visible and apparently only two blocks from us."

At that point, the family soon reached the decision to join the many others thronging the streets and running away from the fire. While some either owned a carriage or cart, others tried in vain to hire one, but as the flames rose, so did the prices, so many were forced to make their way with their trunks and other belongings on their backs. Cassius Wicker was a bachelor and only responsible for his own safety, so he found his escape to be easier than that of many others: "My trunk was soon filled with the most valuable portion of my clothing, etc. and my hand bag packed for a camping out expedition, but all was done quickly and I assure you that I disposed of many an old garment, book and trinket that under other circumstances should not have [been] deserted in their old age. The bottle of brandy…was found while emptying my trunk of worthless trash and safely placed in the bag and it did good service the balance of that night and forenoon at Dick's, and many a stranger took courage from it. After helping my halls chamber girl down, and many another trunk before I could get my own down, I reached the street and started east as the heaviest portion of the fire was not yet there…everybody knew the town was doomed to destruction.

Not surprisingly, Wicker soon realized that the few worldly goods he was able to save were getting heavier by the minute. He explained, "Down to State Street, hailing every man or team for assistance, but all had...theirs to save. Dragging the trunks a block I would set down on it, only to be run over by others equally as anxious as I to get away from the devouring element. Would have given $10 for a rope five feet long--I never knew the value of such a rope until my back was nearly broken and hands so tired I could no longer stir the trunk." Fortunately, help soon arose from an unexpected corner, as he later related: "At last I came to a light wagon with a horse and obtained the assistance of a one-handed man to put the trunk into it, but the owner, or a man stronger than I claimed it. But my one-handed man would work for money and away we went, quite bravely until I could no longer lift my end. We rested more than we walked. Soon I could not stir my end and had a handkerchief through the handle and around my arm. This worked well until…both gave out entirely. Soon an Englishman, fleeing from the wrath,...in a large U.S. Express wagon, himself as motive power, with a few household goods and a sick wife came slowly along. I saw he was about exhausted and could not hold out much longer, so speedily compromised with him--adding our two loads together as well as our united strength, and the way we did the jackass business…"

Of course, only a small number of any person's belongings could be saved, so people made choices, leaving behind expensive oil paintings in favor of old daguerreotypes of dead relatives and wearing heavy wool coats instead of soft silk shawls. Likewise, beautiful churches were blown up in the hope of saving simple homes and offices. There would never be any way of knowing the full value of all the property lost, but there are a few records of some of the most mourned artwork and architecture. Wicker spoke of the losses, as well as the brave work of some who risked everything to save what they could: "The magnificent painting 16 by 32 feet of the Baron of Gillingsbury just behind the hotel was burned about this time. Hurrying to Dick's after seeing church after church, stone block after block blown up in vain endeavor to save what remained and after seeing the flames come from Dick's store, Pullman Palace Car Co. Building, and the Union Depot, we had just time to kick the fine pictures from their frames, load two wagons and be off up the avenue amid fire engines, everybody's last team and crowds of departing homeless people. Not until the flames came into the dining room and leaped over the roof did we leave the house. Never did I work as hard as for the last team--never did I see the avenue so full, to say nothing of crazy people. Never did I see such a wind carrying flames across the broad avenue."

Of course, even the best efforts of people to protect their valuables often failed. Many larger businesses during that era stored their receipts and record books in safes, many of which were supposed to be fireproof, so rather than carry large sums of money and bonds on them, many of the wealthier citizens of the town chose instead to lock these items, along with fine jewelry and other small but valuable possessions, in these safes and leave them behind. This strategy often proved to be a mistake, as Francis Test later explained: "The iron safes stood the heat well, but many were burned to a white heat; their contents were destroyed. I can safely say over two thirds of them were found to contain nothing but charred masses of what once were thousands in bonds and notes…Large safes may be seen walled in at a height of three and four stories. Some of the walls tell the place where a safe once was. The intense heat had made loose the bricks around them and they fell bursting or jammed in such a way that the fire searched out their contents. Many a man has awaited, buoyant with hope, the cooling and opening of his safe, and very many have been disappointed--thousands and thousands of dollars have been taken out charred and burned. I have seen safes completely melted and by one tap of the hammer would crumble like mortar. This fire has taught many lessons, especially in regard to iron safes and fire proof buildings."

Chapter 7: Order

The ruins of Wood's Museum

Picture of a poster from October 10 asking for food

"With the close of the fire, or rather conflagration, our troubles have not closed. Roughs and thieves from all parts of the country flocked here for plunder. Many fires have been started, but in most cases the party caught in the act has been shot on the spot. Their hopes were to burst open the safes, of which there are thousands through the burned district, but Gen. Sheridan promulgated a Death Proclamation to everybody found on the burnt district after dark. Thinking Milwaukee would be off their guard, many started for that city and we put them off the train when, for the sake of plunder, they attempted to throw a train off the track, but so far without success. Every block in the city is guarded strongly by the citizens. As an instance of our quiet times, Wednesday night while on watch between 8 & 2, I heard but 19 shots fired. Many, I hope, were false alarms, but it shows what little mercy is shown." - Cassius Wicker

As important as it was that the fire be put out, the city leaders also understood it was imperative for everyone's health and safety that order be restored. To that end, they made the following proclamation on Monday afternoon as the fire finally began to burn itself out:

- ❖ WHEREAS, In the Providence of God, to whose will we humbly submit, a terrible calamity has befallen our city, which demands of us our best efforts for the preservation of order and relief of suffering, be it known that the faith and credit of the City of Chicago is hereby pledged for the necessary expenses for the relief of the suffering.
- ❖ Public order will be preserved. The police and special police now being appointed will be responsible for the maintenance of the peace and protection of property.
- ❖ All officers and men of the Fire Department and Health Department will act as special policemen without further notice.
- ❖ The Mayor and Comptroller will give vouchers for all supplies furnished by the different relief committees.
- ❖ The headquarters of the City Government will be at the Congregational Church, corner of West Washington and Ann Streets.
- ❖ All persons are warned against any act tending to endanger property. Persons caught in any depredation will be immediately arrested.
- ❖ With the help of God, order and peace and private property will be preserved.
- ❖ The City Government and the committee of citizens pledge themselves to the community to protect them, and prepare the way for a restoration of public and private welfare.
- ❖ It is believed the fire has spent its force, and all will soon be well.

Damage on Washington St.

Though the fire finally burned itself out, aided by a light rain on Monday night, the city was still in great danger. The rain was not enough to thoroughly wet the buildings, and there was still no more water to be had. As Francis Test wrote, "We have the fire departments from all the larger cities in the West but the water has not been introduced into the pipes sufficient to put out the smallest fire. Water is being forced into the mains from the river by the fire engines. They have laid four inch mains above ground to a great distance on the South Side and the water is forced into them by the same means."

As a result, harsh laws against kindling any fire were put into effect. Not only were they enforced by the police officers and other government officials, they were also enforced by the citizens themselves, often with tragic results. As Test wrote, "The city is not strictly under martial law but it reminds me of the first days of the rebellion. Soldiers march our streets; the citizens are patrolling the squares; every alley is guarded and woe be to him that lights a match or smokes a cigar on the street after nightfall. Those who have this matter in charge will not permit any such thing. Fires in the house were prohibited for a long time but the rule is not so strictly observed now as it was. There have been a few men killed and I only wonder that the number is not greater, so intensely excited are the people. Some who have been shot deserved their fate, others were not guilty but indiscreet."

Fortunately, rain came again on Wednesday evening, giving people hope and much needed relief. Test continued, "It commenced raining last night and it is a Godsend. We have caught a supply of water, enough to do washing…The people of the West Side get water from Union Park. There is a small ornamental lake there, but this is fed by the water mains and was almost dipped out till the fire engines began forcing the water from the river into it. On the South Side they have the Lake and as I have said they are conveying water by means of a four inch main around the destroyed property and for a distance beyond."

Nonetheless, the water was only a drop in the bucket toward meeting the needs of the citizens, many of whom were in frightful condition and also needed food and shelter. As always during a disaster, there were those who wanted to take advantage of the situation with price gauging, but they were quickly and harshly dealt with. Test recalled, "I saw a farmer's wagon standing near a market store. It was loaded with bagged beans and a calf. He offered the beans at an exorbitant price and the calf he wanted $50.00 for. A crowd gathered around him and drove him from the city. It was with difficulty he got away unharmed."

Another need that had to be met was for care for the sick and injured. O.W. Clapp was charged with trying to organize locations suitable for medical care and later wrote, "It was there, and then I learned the usefulness of church basements for hospital uses, whereupon I ordered signs to be put on all churches south of the burnt district pointing to the next church basement south for food, beds and clothing. Within a few days all church basements on the south side acted as hospitals, as well as the hospitals and many schoolhouses and private homes." Fortunately, there were many others who just wanted to help, and Test praised these generous souls when he wrote, "Our sister cities are sending us food and everything we want. If it were not for this aid God knows what we should do. Provisions are plentiful and they are being properly disbursed."

In fact, a committee was soon organized to manage the donations being received. A poster informed the public, "J.W. Preston, Esq., President of the Board of Trade, is hereby authorized to receive on account of this Committee, all supplies for the relief of the destitute, and distribute the same to depots of supplies established in the city, under the control and upon the order of this Committee. He is also authorized to hire or press into service, if necessary, a sufficient number of teams to handle such supplies."

Chapter 8: Survival

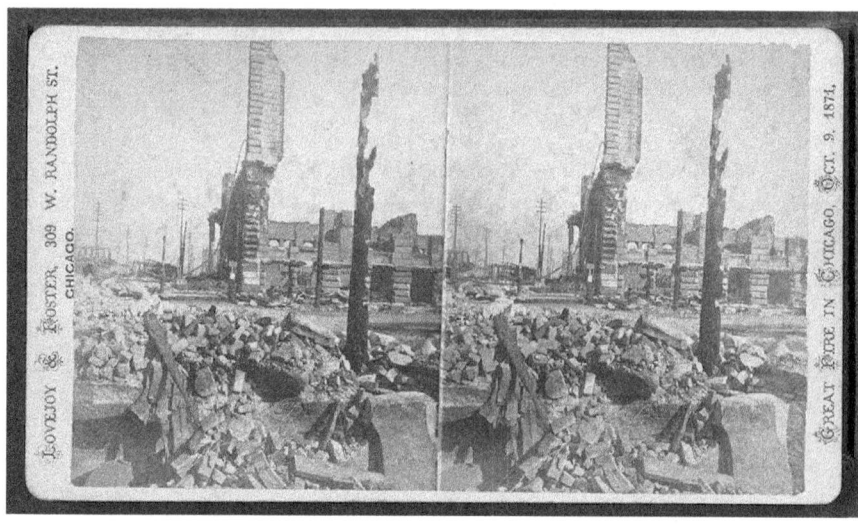

The remains of Chicago's Chamber of Commerce

Damage on Michigan Ave. in the northwestern section

"Having nothing of our own at stake, we could perhaps look on more coolly than some others.

I remember being impressed at the time with the different phases of character so suddenly unveiled. The dear friends who so kindly sheltered us in our extremity, and who, for the last time, threw open those hospitable doors, not to friends merely, but to strangers as well--feeding the hungry, helping and sympathizing with those whose trials seemed greater than they could bear; those friends who looked on calmly as the devouring flames approached their beautiful dwelling, showing plainly that their treasure was laid up in a better country, where they looked for "a house not made with hands." Some came there, trembling and fearful, wholly broken-down, as it were, with their own grief; some came professedly to help--really to pilfer; but the majority were calm, earnest, resolute helpers…" - Mrs. Alfred Hebard

With food and water in place, the third concern for the surviving refugees was shelter, which was a dire situation since cities could not simply provide people places to live as they did with food. Furthermore, it was October, so the days and nights in Chicago were quite cold. Wicker described the first terrible night after the fire: "It's fearful. All down through Lake Park people were strung out on their few things saved, many of them fast asleep with the sand blowing over them…All day long, part of the night before and in many cases, Monday night, hundreds and thousands of people lay out on the sand in the wind strong enough to blow a chair left alone clear across the park. The air was so full of dust and sand that it was impossible to see the fire, and there, utterly exhausted, lay the lowly and the proud."

Unfortunately, at least one businessman thought he could make a profit off of people's misfortune, but according to Test, he quickly learned otherwise: "General Sheridan has control here now and this has done much to stay the confidence of the people. He is a little God here. Hotel and boarding housekeepers were trying to make money out of the misfortunes of the people. Sheridan went to one of our hotels, asked the proprietor what he asked for room and board per day. 'I am charging $10.00, sir. Will you register your name?' 'No sir, but I will inform you that if you cannot give room and board at $3.00 per day I can find someone that can. I suppose you understand that.'"

Fortunately, by Tuesday morning, help had been put in place for those left destitute by the fire. A public notice informed them, "The headquarters of the General Relief Committee are at the Congregational Church, corner of Washington and Ann streets. All of the public school buildings, as well as churches, are open for the shelter of persons who do not find other accommodations. When food is not found at such buildings, it will be provided by the committee on application headquarters." Moreover, the city did not have to provide shelter for everyone because some were able to find housing elsewhere in the area. Julia Lemos explained, "[F]ather told me that the government was giving free passes on the railroads, so people could go to their friends and that he could take us to New York to my aunt there. As all the firms I worked for were burned I knew it would be very long before I would have work to support the family, but might get work in New York, so I told father to get the pass and we would go. The next morning he went after the pass…Well how were we to get to the train for New York? There was no way--

so the janitor of the church had a wagon and horse, and offered, if father would let him have the dog … he would take us to the train, in his wagon, so father arranged it, and he put our two trunks in the wagon then we got in…"

The railroads did indeed offer free passes to people, but they soon had to limit the policy to only women and children since the men were needed to help with repairing the city. The fire had destroyed more than 120 miles of sidewalk and 70 miles of road, and 2,000 lampposts were gone, leaving the city in eerie darkness each evening. A third of the city's buildings were gone, and more than 100,000 people left homeless.

Considering all the damage, the estimated death toll of close to 300 was surprisingly low, and Frederick Olmsted found the number so low that he mentioned it in his writings: "That the number should be small can only be accounted for by the fact that there was an active volunteer rear-guard of cool-headed Christians, who often entered and searched houses to which they were strangers, dragging out their inmates sometimes by main force, and often when some, caught unawares, were bewildered, fainting, or suffocating." He continued praising those left in Chicago, writing, "For a time men were unreasonably cheerful and hopeful; now, this stage appears to have passed. In its place there is sternness; but so narrow is the division between this and another mood, that in the midst of a sentence a change of quality in the voice occurs, and you see that eyes have moistened. I had partly expected to find a feverish, reckless spirit, and among the less disciplined classes an unusual current setting towards turbulence, lawlessness, and artificial jollity, such as held in San Francisco for a long time after the great fire there--such as often seizes seamen after a wreck. On the contrary, Chicago is the soberest and the most clear headed city I ever saw. I have observed but two men the worse for liquor; I have not once been asked for an alms, nor have I heard a hand-organ. The clearing of the wreck goes ahead in a driving but steady, well-ordered way. I have seen two hundred brick walls rising, ten thousand temporary houses of boards, and fifty thousand piles of materials lifting from the ruins…"

There was a good reason why Olmsted observed so little drunkenness; during the days following the fire, the city's first order was "that no liquor be sold in any Saloon," and the city later decreed, "All saloons are ordered to be closed at 9 P.M. every day for one week, under a penalty of forfeiture of license."

Chapter 9: Protection

"There was a crowd in the middle of the street dragging a man along with a rope around his neck, they were going to hang him, he had been caught setting fire for robbery, that frightened me, and I said we will leave Chicago at once, I would be afraid to have my children on the street. The second night at the church every one was asleep at midnight, but on account of my baby being restless, I woke up, and saw a rough looking man coming in the church door, I pretended to be asleep but watched him, he laid down in a pew for a while, then he rose up and looked about to see if he was observed, a man laid asleep in the next pew, and he reached over and was just taking his watch, when I set up and the thief started and laid down again, I pretended to wait on baby, but whispered to mother to tell father, which she did, and as father was an old soldier and had a gun, he with several others were appointed a guard in the church, he went to the others and called them, and they closed about the man and took him to a guardhouse they had about there." - Julia Lemos

Determined to protect the citizens in his community, Mayor Mason issued a notice as the fire was dying down that the city would be divided into districts and that each district would recruit 500 citizens to act as Special Policemen. Furthermore, he announced, "The Military are invested with full Police power, and will be respected and obeyed in their efforts to preserve order." In effect, he declared martial law and put General Philip Sheridan, a Union hero during the Civil War, in charge of keeping order in the city. Charles Holden later wrote, "For two weeks Sheridan oversaw a de facto martial law of dubious legitimacy implemented by a mix of regular troops, militia units, police, and a specially organized 'First Regiment of Chicago Volunteers.' They patrolled the streets, guarded the relief warehouses, and enforced curfews and other regulations. John DeKoven, cashier of the Merchants' National Bank of Chicago, wrote to his wife of his experience as a sentry, 'I have not had my clothes off for a week, the city is patrolled every night, you should have seen me last night patrolling our alley with a loaded revolver in my hand looking for incendiaries for there are many about.' Illinois Governor Richard Oglesby, among others, strongly questioned whether such measures were justified and legal, but the calming effect of Mason's actions in the days right after the fire was evident, especially among the well-to-do. Former Lieutenant-Governor William Bross, part owner of the Tribune, later recollected his response to the arrival of Sheridan's soldiers: 'Never did deeper emotions of joy overcome me. Thank God, those most dear to me and the city as well are safe.'"

Illustration depicting the ruins of the National Bank of Chicago

Sheridan

Unfortunately, the citizen police officers were not thoroughly trained in handling difficult situations like the police often encountered. In fact, they were not really trained at all. Many were former Union soldiers who had fought in the Civil War and as such had developed a certain willingness to shoot at a fellow American that many past and future generations would find hard to understand. Others had fought in the Indian Wars and had not fired a gun in decades. Still others had never been in any kind of organized conflict and had no clue how to give and take orders. The only thing that the mayor could hope for was that most were armed with some sort of common sense.

O.W. Clapp was one of those deputized, and he made the following observation about his service, which centered primarily on the first wave of food distribution: "Mayor Mason then clothed me with a lead pencil order on the back of an old envelope and a Policeman's star and a verbal order to act on my own responsibility and not bother him. I proceeded to ask the views of those I thought my peers in this emergency and visited certain sections of the south side driving through parts of the burnt district...Next morning ... I went to the Plymouth Congregational Church, corner Wabash Ave. and Eldridge Court and found Rev. Wm. Alvin Bartlett at breakfast and applied to him for men in the basement of his church to go with me to the Warehouse and help unload cars and load wagons... The Doctor at once went to the basement of his church, mounting a chair called for recruits to aid the distribution. About 20 men volunteered... Coming out we saw one of Farwells, and one of Fields big truck wagons. I ordered the driver to take these men on their trucks to the 18th St. warehouse, near the river. They rebelled, but soon repented being persuaded by the minister and men and my showing of a police star."

As the weeks wore on, there was more and more to protect and distribute. Towns from around the state and cities from around the country began to send donations to Chicagoans. New York City send food, clothing and $450,000 in cash, while Milwaukee, St. Louis, Cleveland, Buffalo and Cincinnati provided hundreds of thousands of dollars worth of money and goods. Even London, on the other side of the world, sent more than £7,000 to Chicago. To his credit, Mason was sensitive to the need to manage these donations well and formed yet another committee. As Holden pointed out, "The Relief and Aid Society's fire activities were considerably more long-lived, extending into 1874. Dividing the city into districts, the Society opened offices and supply depots connected by telegraph. It separated its work into different areas--contributions, shelter, employment, transportation, distribution, and health--each overseen by a designated committee. The Society not only distributed food and clothing, but also made available the materials for several thousand simple 'shelter houses,' erected four barracks in different places throughout the city for the homeless poor, helped secure necessary tools and appliances to skilled workers, and vaccinated tens of thousands of Chicagoans against smallpox. Its work was a model of a new kind of 'scientific' charity, conducted by paid professionals carrying out the policies of an executive board."

Chapter 10: Rebuilding

> **CHEER UP.**
> In the midst of a calamity without parallel in the world's history, looking upon the ashes of thirty years' accumulations, the people of this once beautiful city have resolved that
> **CHICAGO SHALL RISE AGAIN**

Part of an article in *The Chicago Tribune* after the fire

"You ask whether it is in the power of man adequately to guard against such calamities-- whether other great cities are as much exposed as was Chicago. All the circumstances are not established with sufficient accuracy for a final answer, and one cannot, in the present condition of affairs, make full enquiries of men who must be best informed; but to such preliminary discussion as is in order, I can only offer a certain contribution. (…) No one can be sure that with reasonably solid brick walls, reasonably good construction, and honest architecture, this fire could, once under strong headway, with the wind that was blowing, have been stopped at any point in its career, even by good generalship, directing a thoroughly well-drifted and disciplined soldierly force of fireman and police. But that the heat thrown forward would have been less intense, the advance of the fire less rapid, the destruction of buildings less complete, the salvage of their contents greater, and the loss of life smaller, may be assumed with confidence." - Frederick Olmsted

Fanny Boggs Lester was 11 when Chicago burned, and she recorded her memories in a letter written about 75 years later: "Opposite us on the S.E. corner of Michigan Ave. and Twenty-third was a vacant lot. When we looked out in the morning it was filled with refugees from the hotels with their belongings in bags, sheets and pillow cases. In front of our house was a hearse filled with baggage and on the driver's seat a man with his marble mantle clock. I remember my mother saying, 'I certainly would not have chosen that heavy thing to carry,' so as one of the letters said 'there were amusing things too.' I remember my mother with others feeding these sufferers, in the Michigan Ave. Baptist Church which was two doors from us, and for many following weeks, because a distributing center to give out clothing and food that came so generously from many places. The danger from incendiary fires made my father and the other residents of our blocks watch night after night. One was discovered near us. I to help, got my new shoes and put all the silver and napkins in these and was ready to go. For weeks we had to use candles which mother put in bottles with water in them and card-board to catch the wax. When my father let me ride down with him to see the wreck the cedar blocks of the pavement were still smoking in many places which our horse did not like..."

As is always the case with a tragedy, the story is not complete until someone has been blamed. While this seems cruel and mean-spirited, there is also a practical reason for establishing blame, because if people can determine what went wrong in the situation, there is hope that corrections can be made in the future and that such a hardship will not have to be experienced again. One of the first reports issued about what could have prevented the fire, or at least minimized its damage, came from those at the forefront of fighting it. The official report of the board of the Chicago Fire Department observed, "We believe that had the buildings on the West Side, where the fire commenced, been built of brick or stone, with safe roofings (the buildings need not have been fire-proof) the fire could have been stopped without great danger, and certainly would not have crossed the river. After it did cross, the wooden cornices, wooden signs of large size, the cupolas, and the tar and felt roofs, which were on most of the best buildings, caused their speedy destruction, and aided greatly in spreading the conflagration." The board then went on to add, "The single set of pumping works, upon which the salvation of the city depended, were roofed with wood, had no appliance by which water could be raised to the roof in case of fire, and was one of the earliest buildings to burn in the North Division."

In order to bolster its case, the board went on to point out, "The Board of Police have, year by year, in annual reports to the Mayor and Common Council, endeavored to point out the great defects of the manner in which our city was being built up. We advised and entreated before such an immense amount of combustibles was piled around the heart of the city. We reported mansard and tar roofs to be unsafe; that the water supply was insufficient; that our fire hydrants were twice too far apart; that we ought to have Fire Department cisterns at the intersections of the streets, so that we should always have water at fires; that we ought to have floating fire engines, with powerful pumps, in the river, to enable the firemen to wet down fifteen hundred feet on either side of the river or its branches; that wooden cornices were an abomination; that the Holly system of pumping the water and sending it through the pipes, with a pressure of forty pounds on ordinary occasions, with power to increase it to one hundred pounds in case of fire, would give us four sets of pumping works in different parts of the city, and not leave us to the mercy of chance, or, accident, with a single set."

Of course, the changes suggested in the report would have been expensive, and then as now, small local governments were reluctant to spend the money to make the upgrades. Also, the Civil War had ended a mere six years earlier, and the entire country was in the midst of a post-war economic crisis that even affected growing cities like Chicago. That said, the report was quick to point out the flaw in the "costs too much" excuse: "We showed that the four sets of Holly works could be built for less than one year's interest on the cost of the present Water Works, and, when built, would admit of the dispensing with every engine in the Fire Department where the water was in the street, allowing us to get rid of most of the horses and all the engines of the Department, and to reduce the number of men one-half--saving two-thirds of the expense of the Fire Department, and making it as efficient as it would be with one hundred steam fire engines."

Having gotten the readers' attention, the authors of the report then went in for the kill, writing: "None of these things was noticed by the mayor, the Common Council, or the newspapers. No heed being paid to our suggestions, so far as any improvement of our plan of extinguishing fires was concerned, the only thing we could do was to ask for an increase of the engine companies, in order that we might be prepared as well as possible to contend with the great fires to which we were and are still liable." They closed with a summary of their concerns: "Our engines have always been too few in number and too far apart. The Fire Department should be very much enlarged, or the system of putting out fires by steam engines be abandoned. If the citizens do not believe this now, they will after the next great fire sweeps out of existence the greater portion of the wooden city which now remains."

This time, the city leaders listened. Within weeks of the fire, committees began to draft new laws concerning where and how new buildings could be built. They also consulted fire prevention expert Arthur C. Ducat and others on how to reform the fire department. Before long, the Chicago Fire Department earned a reputation for being one of the best fire departments in the United States.

Meanwhile, Gordon Hubbard, who had sheltered the Hebard's and many others until his own home burned, threw his money and efforts into rebuilding the city. In fact, he ordered lumber delivered to town before the last fire had even gone out. Francis Test also tried to assure those he was writing to: "The heart of our city is gone, but our business men are not discouraged. Soon we will begin again. Even now over the smoldering ruins they are placing new buildings. Our houses may be burned but our energies are just the same, they cannot be destroyed. It looks like rain tonight. The clouds are very dark and on these the light from the burning coal heaps reflect a living red that is surely visible for miles. We have the fire departments from all the larger cities in the West but the water has not been introduced into the pipes sufficient to put out the smallest fire. Water is being forced into the mains from the river by the fire engines. They have laid four inch mains above ground to a great distance on the South Side and the water is forced into them by the same means."

Mayor Mason, who saw the city through its darkest days, stayed on to help with the rebuilding, but not as mayor. He was soon replaced in office by his successor, Joseph Medill, and less than two weeks after the fire, he issued his last order related to the incident: "In view of the recent appalling public calamity, the undersigned, Mayor of Chicago, hereby earnestly recommends that all the inhabitants of this city do observe Sunday, October 29, as a special day of humiliation and prayer; of humiliation for those past offenses against Almighty God, to which these severe afflictions were doubtless intended to lead our minds; of prayer for the relief and comfort of the suffering thousands in our midst; for the restoration of our material prosperity, especially for our lasting improvements as a people in reverence and obedience to God. Nor should we even, amidst our losses and sorrows, forget to render thanks to Him for the arrest of the devouring fires in time to save so many homes, and for the unexampled sympathy and aid which has flowed in upon us from every quarter of our land, and even from beyond the seas."

Picture of a sculpture commemorating the site where the fire started

Bibliography

Bales, Richard F. (2002). *The Great Chicago Fire and the Myth of Mrs. O'Leary's Cow.* Jefferson, NC.: McFarland.

Chicago and the Great Conflagration – Elias Colbert and Everett Chamberlin, 1871, 528 pp.

"Who Caused the Great Chicago Fire? A Possible Deathbed Confession" – by Anthony DeBartolo, *Chicago Tribune*, October 8, 1997 and "Odds Improve That a Hot Game of Craps in Mrs. O'Leary's Barn Touched Off Chicago Fire" – by Anthony DeBartolo, *Chicago Tribune*,

March 3, 1998

"History of the Great Fires in Chicago and the West". – Rev. Edgar J. Goodspeed, D.D., 677 pp.

The Great Conflagration – James W. Sheahan and George P. Upton 1871, 458 pp.

Smith, Carl (1995). *Urban Disorder and the Shape of Belief: The Great Chicago Fire, the Haymarket Bomb, and the Model Town of Pullman.* Chicago, Ill.: University of Chicago Press.

"Mrs. O'Leary's Comet: Cosmic Causes of the Great Chicago Fire" by Mel Waskin (Jan 1985)

The Peshtigo Fire

Chapter 1: A Source of Prosperity

An 1867 picture of a Peshtigo saw mill

A Peshtigo factory

"Peshtigo is situated on a river of that name, about six miles from Green Bay with which it communicates by means of a small railroad. The Company established at Peshtigo is a source of prosperity to the whole country, not only from its spirit of enterprise and large pecuniary resources but also from its numerous establishments, the most important of which, a factory of tubs and buckets, affords alone steady employment to more than three hundred workmen. The population of Peshtigo, including the farmers settled in the neighborhood, numbered then about two thousand souls. We were just finishing the construction of a church looked on as a great embellishment to the parish." – Reverend Peter Pernin, *The Great Peshtigo Fire: An Eyewitness Account*

In the days following the dreadful fire in Peshtigo, Wisconsin, most of the town's inhabitants were too stunned and too upset to write about their recollections. Few reporters even bothered to interview the survivors to get a firsthand account of what occurred that night because the world was so obsessed with the events that had occurred that same evening in nearby Chicago. Even as the months passed and the citizens of Peshtigo began to rebuild their lives, the curious passed quickly through the site of the worst fire in American history to get to the site of the most famous one. For the most part, the fire and the people involved were largely ignored.

However, there was one man in Peshtigo that night who refused to let the story of what he saw go untold. Father Peter Pernin was an itinerant priest serving both the Catholics in Peshtigo and those in nearby Marinette. His story would provide the only complete eyewitness account of what occurred that night, and the accounts of others also serve as an invitation for readers to revisit that dreadful night in history.

Father Pernin, in recalling the landscape around Peshtigo, Wisconsin, wrote, "A country covered with dense forests, in the midst of which are to be met with here and there, along newly opened roads, clearings of more or less extent, sometimes a half league in width to afford space for an infant town, or perhaps three or four acres intended for a farm. With the exception of these isolated spots where the trees have been cut down and burned, all is a wild but majestic forest. Trees, trees everywhere, nothing else but trees as far as you can travel from the bay, either towards the north or west. These immense forests are bounded on the east by Green Bay of Lake Michigan, and by the lake itself. The face of the country is in general undulating, diversified by valleys overgrown with cedars and spruce trees, sandy hills covered with evergreens, and large tracts of rich land filled with the different varieties of hard wood, oak, maple, beech, ash, elm, and birch. The climate of this region is generally uniform and favorable to the crops that are now tried there with remarkable success. Rains are frequent, and they generally fall at a favorable time."

Unlike the Chicago fire, there is no creative legend surrounding Peshtigo's conflagration; it simply was a tragic combination of bad weather and bad behavior. Pernin was inclined to put more emphasis on the latter than the former in determining blame for what came later. He explained, "The year 1871 was, however, distinguished by its unusual dryness. Farmers had profited of the latter circumstance to enlarge their clearings, cutting down and burning the wood that stood in their way. Hundreds of laborers employed in the construction of a railroad had acted in like manner, availing themselves of both axe and fire to advance their work. Hunters and Indians scour these forests continually… At night they kindle a large fire wherever they may chance to halt … knowing that the fire will keep at a distance any wild animals that may happen to range through the vicinity during the night. The ensuing morning they depart without taking the precaution of extinguishing the smoldering embers of the fire that has protected and warmed them … If fanned by a brisk gale of wind they are liable to assume most formidable proportions. Twice or thrice before October 8, the effects of the wind, favored by the general dryness, had filled the inhabitants of the environs with consternation."

To be fair, a lack of responsibility was not the only explanation offered for the fiery disaster. In 1883, scientist Ignatius Donnelly made a compelling argument postulating that all of the fires in the area that night were caused by a meteor shower created when Biela's Comet lost its tail. In defending his theory, he wrote, "At that hour, half past nine o'clock in the evening, at apparently the same moment, at points hundreds of miles apart, in three different States, Wisconsin, Michigan, and Illinois, fires of the most peculiar and devastating kind broke out, so far as we know, by spontaneous combustion. In Wisconsin, on its eastern borders, in a heavily timbered country, near Lake Michigan, a region embracing four hundred square miles, extending north from Brown County, and containing Peshtigo, Manistee, Holland, and numerous villages on the shores of Green Bay, was swept bare by an absolute whirlwind of flame. There were seven hundred and fifty people killed outright, besides great numbers of the wounded, maimed, and burned, who died afterward. More than three million dollars' worth of property was destroyed."

While the meteorite explanation still has a number of defenders, it has never gained widespread popularity in the scientific community, primarily because it would be impossible for a meteor to retain enough heat under normal atmospheric conditions to start a fire. That said, there was nothing normal about the conditions in the Midwest that fall, since the area was at the height of a severe drought that had plagued farmers throughout the summer of 1871. Meteorologists recorded only one inch of rainfall between July 4 and the day of the fire. This had dried up the swamps around the town and had caused the leaves on the deciduous trees to shed their leaves early. These leaves, in turn, dried out quickly, producing more tinder just waiting to be ignited. One Midwesterner noted, "This season has been the dryest in the West for years. We hadn't had a drop of rain for months, and there had been but one cloudy day during the month of September. The result was that the dust was almost intolerable, the ground became parched, and the houses were as dry as tinder. Besides a furious wind from the southwest had been blowing steadily all day Sunday, one of the most violent winds I ever saw in a clear day."

It was this wind that would turn the fire from a mishap into a disaster.

Chapter 2: Two Different Impressions

Picture of the Peshtigo dock on Green Bay

"In the outer world everything contributed to keep alive these two different impressions. On one side, the thick smoke darkening the sky, the heavy, suffocating atmosphere, the mysterious silence filling the air, so often a presage of storm, seemed to afford grounds for fear in case of a sudden gale. On the other hand the passing and repassing in the street of countless young people bent only on amusement, laughing, singing, and perfectly indifferent to the menacing aspect of nature, was sufficient to make me think that I alone was a prey to anxiety, and to render me ashamed of manifesting the feeling." - Reverend Peter Pernin, *The Great Peshtigo Fire: An Eyewitness Account*

It appears that the fire first began outside of town, in a nearby forest area. For days, farmers and others went out to fight the fire, but little could be done. In late September, one man wrote the following: "Sunday, the 24th inst., was an exciting, I might say a fearful time, in Peshtigo. For several days the fires had been raging in the timber all around--north, south, east, and west. Saturday the flames burned through to the river a little above the town; and on Saturday night, much danger was apprehended from the sparks and cinders that blew across the river, into the upper part of the town, near the factory. A force was stationed along the river, and although fire caught in the sawdust and dry slabs it was promptly extinguished. It was a grand sight, the fire that night. It burned to the tops of the tallest trees, enveloped them in a mantle of flames, or, winding itself about them like a huge serpent, crept to their summits, out upon the branches, and wound its huge folds about them. Hissing and glaring it lapped out its myriad fiery tongues while its fierce breath swept off the green leaves and roared through the forest like a tempest."

The author of this quote obviously had a flair for the dramatic, but he was correct in his assessment of the fight to halt the fire outside of the town. He continued, "Sunday morning the fires had died down, so that we began to hope the danger was over. About eleven o'clock … the steam whistle of the factory blew a wild blast of alarm. In a moment the temples were emptied of their worshippers, the latter rushing wildly out to see what had happened."

It soon became all too clear what had happened, but this time it proved to be only a warning about the greater danger to come: "Fire had caught in the sawdust near the factory again, but before we reached the spot it was extinguished. The wind had suddenly risen and was blowing a gale from the northwest. The fires in the timber were burning more fiercely than ever, and were approaching the river directly opposite the factory. …everything that was possible was done to prevent the fire from entering the town. But now a new danger arose. The fires to the west of the town were approaching rapidly, and it seemed that nothing short of a miracle could save it from utter destruction. A cloud of hot, blinding smoke blew in our faces and made it extremely difficult to see or do anything; still prompt and energetic means were taken to check the approaching flames."

At first, it seemed like the great fire was upon the town, but it wasn't, at least not just yet. As the anonymous author wrote, "Monday, the wind veered to the south, and cleared away the smoke. Strange to say not a building was burned--the town was saved. Monday the factory was closed to give the men rest, and today, September 27, all is quiet and going on as usual." Nonetheless, fires continued to spring up around the countryside over the next few weeks.

Decades later, Mary Keith wrote about the story her parents had told her about the fire: "It had been a very dry season, and I recall my mother telling us several times of the fire that for about two weeks before the sun was obscured, the clothes on the line looked so gray, and a kind of foreboding feeling that something was going to happen hung over the city. She said the fire came so suddenly that the only way she could describe it was that the heavens opened up and it rained fire. I think the fact that they were on the outskirts of the city was the only thing that saved them. I was nearly a year old when it happened."

Since it was easier to see the approach of the conflagration out in the country, as long as the fire remained outside the city, no lives were lost. However, every day brought new concerns. While those who could went into the woods to fight the blaze, those who could not do such work remained in their homes, preparing for the worst while praying for the best. One person later described the scene to a reporter who wrote about it for a nearby newspaper: "Sunday evening, after church, for about half an hour a death like stillness hung over the doomed town. The smoke from the fires in the region around, was so thick as to be stifling and hung like a funeral pall over everything and all was enveloped in Egyptian darkness. Soon, light puffs of air were felt, the horizon at the south east, south and south west began to be faintly illuminated, a perceptible trembling of the earth was felt, and a distant roar broke the awful silence. People began to fear that some awful calamity was impending, but as yet, no one even dreamed of the danger. The illumination soon became intensified into a fierce lurid glare, the roar deepened into a howl, as if all the demons from the infernal pit had been let loose, when the advance gusts of wind from the main body … struck."

Chapter 3: The Crimson Reflection, the Muttered Thunder

"The crimson reflection in the western portion of the sky was rapidly increasing in size and in intensity; then between each stroke of my pickax I heard plainly, in the midst of the unnatural calm and silence reigning around, the strange and terrible noise already described, the muttered thunder of which became more distinct as it drew each moment nearer. This sound resembled the confused noise of a number of cars and locomotives approaching a railroad station, or the rumbling of thunder, with the difference that it never ceased, but deepened in intensity each moment more and more. The spectacle of this menacing crimson in the sky, the sound of this strange and unknown voice of nature constantly augmenting in terrible majesty, seemed to endow me with supernatural strength. Whilst toiling thus steadfastly at my task, the sound of human voices plainly audible amid the silence and species of stupor reigning around fell on my ear. They betrayed on the one hand thoughtlessness, on the other folly." - Reverend Peter Pernin, *The Great Peshtigo Fire: An Eyewitness Account*

Among those both praying and preparing during the early days of October was Father Pernin. He was at his church in Peshtigo on Sunday, October 8th and recalled, "During the afternoon, an old Canadian, remarkable for the deep interest he always took in everything relating to the church, came and asked permission to dig a well close to the sacred edifice so as to have water ready at hand in case of accident, as well as for the use of the plasterer who was coming to work the following morning. As my petitioner had no time to devote to the task during the course of the week, I assented. His labor completed, he informed me there was abundance of water, adding with an expression of deep satisfaction: 'Father, not for a large sum of money would I give that well. Now if a fire breaks out again it will be easy to save our church.'"

Though the well gave both the parishioner and the priest some sense of security, that sense would soon prove false. In the meanwhile, the good father had the care of the souls in his charge to attend to and decided to take some time on that Sunday evening to visit a parishioner whom he knew lived on the side of the town where the fire was most fiercely burning. It was while walking outside with her to take a look at the woods burning in the distance that he got his first sense of how much danger they were really in. He noted, "Towards seven in the evening, always haunted by the same misgivings, I left home to see how it went with my neighbors. ... At one time, whilst we were still in the fields, the wind rose suddenly with more strength than it had yet displayed and I perceived some old trunks of trees blaze out though without seeing about them any tokens of cinder or spark, just as if the wind had been a breath of fire, capable of kindling them into a flame by its mere contact. We extinguished these; the wind fell again, and nature resumed her moody and mysterious silence ... On looking towards the west, whence the wind had persistently blown for hours past, I perceived above the dense cloud of smoke overhanging the earth, a vivid red reflection of immense extent, and then suddenly struck on my ear, strangely audible in the preternatural silence reigning around, a distant roaring, yet muffled sound, announcing that the elements were in commotion somewhere. I rapidly resolved to return home and prepare, without further hesitation, for whatever events were impending."

Unlike Chicago, Peshtigo was a small town of less than 2,000 in 1871. Since it was not as built up as the bigger city, nor as crowded, the fire should not have spread as quickly as it did that day. However, there was another factor to be considered: the wind. On the morning of October 8, a cold front moved into the area from the west, bringing strong winds with it. One fireman explained, "The fire must have been burning from ten to fifteen minutes; and with the wind then blowing strongly from the southwest, and carrying the fire from building to building in a neighborhood composed wholly of dry wooden buildings, with wood shavings piled in every barn and under every house.... the strong wind ... scattered the fire into the many buildings, all as dry as tinder, and spread it over so large an area that [they] ... were unable to cut it off or prevent the wind, which soon became a gale, from carrying burning shingles and brands over their heads, and setting on fire buildings far away from the main fire."

The high winds in and around Peshtigo that day quickly produced a firestorm, something one author once described as "nature's nuclear explosion." What passed through Peshtigo that night left the community looking like a war zone. Throughout the early evening, the wind picked up, and with it the fire. G.T. Tisdale later recalled, "During the day-Sabbath-the air was filled with smoke which grew more dense toward evening, and it was noticed that the air, which was quite chilly, during the day, grew quite warm, and hot puffs were quite frequent in the evening. About half past eight o'clock at night we could see there was a heavy fire to the southwest of the town, and a dull roaring sound like that of heavy wind came up from that quarter. At nine o'clock the wind was blowing very fresh, and by half past nine a perfect gale. The roar of the approaching tornado grew more terrible at ten. When the fire struck the town it seemed to swallow up and literally [sic] drown everything. The fire came on swifter than a horse-race, and within twenty minutes of the time it struck the outskirts of the town, everything was in flames."

Chapter 4: Seek the River at Once

"About nine, the company dispersed, and Mrs. Tyler, the hostess, approached me. ...

'Father,' she questioned, 'do you think there is any danger?'

'I do not know,' was my reply, 'but I have unpleasant presentiments, and feel myself impelled to prepare for trouble.'

'But if a fire breaks out, Father, what are we to do?'

'In that case, Madam, seek the river at once.'

I gave her no reason for advising such a course, perhaps I had really none to offer, beyond that it was my innate conviction." - Reverend Peter Pernin, *The Great Peshtigo Fire: An Eyewitness Account*

As the fire approached, people around town understandably became more and more concerned, and many began putting together bundles of valuables that they would be able to carry with them if the fire did indeed reach the city. Mothers woke sleeping children and dressed them warmly for the night air while fathers turned livestock loose with the hope that they would be able to save themselves from the coming catastrophe. Some packed silver, while others took pictures of their ancestors, long dead or killed just a few years earlier during the Civil War.

Meanwhile, back at his church, Father Pernin was making his own preparations. He later wrote, "IT WAS NOW ABOUT half past eight in the evening. I first thought of my horse and turned him free into the street, deeming that, in any case, he would have more chance of escape thus than tied up in the stable. I then set about digging a trench six feet wide and six or seven feet deep, in the sandy soil of the garden, and though the earth was easy enough to work my task proved a tedious one. The atmosphere was heavy and oppressive, strangely affecting the strength and rendering respiration painful and laborious. The only consideration that could have induced me to keep on working when I found it almost impossible to move my limbs, was the fear, growing more strongly each moment into a certainty, that some great catastrophe was approaching"

The first flames of the forest fire, quickly becoming a firestorm, reached the town limits of

Peshtigo at about 9:00 p.m. on Sunday evening. These were not the flames of just one fire but dozens. At this time, many were still in their homes packing, and Father Pernin was putting together the last of the things he felt he must take with him and trying to secure those items he felt he had to leave behind: "After finishing the digging of the trench I placed within it my trunks, books, church ornaments, and other valuables, covering the whole with sand to a depth of about a foot. Whilst still engaged at this, my servant, who had collected in a basket several precious objects in silver committed to my charge, such as crosses, medals, rosaries, etc., ran and deposited them on the steps of a neighboring store, scarcely conscious in her trouble of what she was doing. She hastily returned for a cage containing her canary, which the wind, however, almost immediately tore from her grasp--and breathless with haste and terror she called to me to leave the garden and fly. The wind, forerunner of the tempest, was increasing in violence, the redness in the sky deepening, and the roaring sound like thunder seemed almost upon us."

Soon, the air itself became so hot that it burned as people filled the streets, women carrying babies and dragging along young children while men urged horse drawn carts along. Everyone, it seems, had the same idea as Father Pernin – to get to the river. By this time, G.T. Tisdale was trying to join the fleeing throng, only to learn that it would be easier said than done. He remembered, "What follows beggars all description. About the time the fire reached the Peshtigo House, I ran out at the east door, and, as I stepped on the platform, the wind caught me and hurled me some distance on to my head and shoulders, and blew me on to my face several times on going to the river. Then came a fierce, devouring, pitiless rain of fire and sand, so hot as to ignite everything it touched."

The firestorm had arrived in all its fury, and many were in the midst of it. Scientists would later estimate that the wind that night blew in excess of 100 miles per hour, a speed that would have classified it as a hurricane had it been raining water instead of fire. Some would later explain that what was now approaching the town seemed to be a wall of fire that fed itself with no need of wood for fuel and generating temperatures in excess of 2,000 degrees.

Of course, few had time to stop and study their surroundings or think about the science of the firestorm. However, Father Pernin was later able to describe the way his church looked in the last moments that he saw it standing: "[A] strange and startling phenomenon met my view. It was that of a cloud of sparks that blazed up here and there with a sharp detonating sound like that of powder exploding, and flew from room to room. I understood then that the air was saturated with some special gas, and I could not help thinking if this gas lighted up from mere contact with a breath of hot wind, what would it be when fire would come in actual contact with it ... The lamps were burning on the table, and I thought, as I turned away, how soon their gleam would be eclipsed in the vivid light of a terrible conflagration ... Then I hastened out to open the gate so as to bring forth my wagon. Barely had I laid hand on it, when the wind heretofore violent rose suddenly to a hurricane, and quick as lightning opened the way for my egress from the yard by sweeping planks, gate, and fencing away into space ... I had delayed my departure too long. It would be impossible to describe the trouble I had to keep my feet, to breathe, to retain hold of the buggy which the wind strove to tear from my grasp."

Chapter 5: Near the River

"Arrived near the river, we saw that the houses adjacent to it were on fire, whilst the wind blew the flames and cinders directly into the water. The place was no longer safe. I resolved then to cross to the other side though the bridge was already on fire. The latter presented a scene of indescribable and awful confusion, each one thinking he could attain safety on the other side of the river. Those who lived in the east were hurrying towards the west, and those who dwelt in that west were wildly pushing on to the east so that the bridge was thoroughly encumbered with cattle, vehicles, women, children, and men, all pushing and crushing against each other so as to find an issue from it. Arrived amid the crowd on the other side, I resolved to descend the river, to a certain distance below the dam, where I knew the shore was lower and the water shallower, but this I found impossible." - Reverend Peter Pernin, *The Great Peshtigo Fire: An Eyewitness Account*

It was soon obvious to Father Pernin and everyone else that the fire was moving faster than they could. Even worse, it seemed to be coming from all directions at once. A crowd of people would turn down one street to flee the flames only to see that the buildings a few blocks away were already ablaze. Then, turning quickly, they faced the terrifying spectacle of either trampling their neighbors or being trampled themselves. Even those who had a clear plan in mind were stymied by the heat, wind, and sand blowing at them. Father Pernin wrote, "The air was no longer fit to breathe, full as it was of sand, dust, ashes, cinders, sparks, smoke, and fire. It was almost impossible to keep one's eyes unclosed, to distinguish the road, or to recognize people, though the way was crowded with pedestrians, as well as vehicles crossing and crashing against each other in the general flight. Some were hastening towards the river, others from it, whilst all were struggling alike in the grasp of the hurricane. A thousand discordant deafening noises rose on the air together. The neighing of horses, falling of chimneys, crashing of uprooted trees, roaring and whistling of the wind, crackling of fire as it ran with lightning-like rapidity from house to house--all sounds were there save that of the human voice. People seemed stricken dumb by terror. They jostled each other without exchanging look, word, or counsel. The silence--of the tomb reigned among the living; nature alone lifted up its voice and spoke. Though meeting crowded vehicles taking a direction quite opposite to that which I myself was following, it never even entered my mind that it would perhaps be better for me to follow them. Probably it was the same thing with them. We all hurried blindly on to our fate."

As chaotic as the situation in town was, the situation near the river was actually much worse. One group ran toward the bridge over the river, thinking that they would be safe on the other side, but they soon saw that there was fire on the other side of the river too. In fact, they were confronted with people running toward them from where the fire was burning on their side of town. Then, just as it seemed as if things could not get any worse, the bridge itself began to burn: "Chimneys were blown down, houses were unroofed, the roof of the Wooden Ware Factory was lifted, a large ware house filled with tubs, pails ... and fish kits was nearly demolished, and amid the confusion terror and terrible apprehension of the moment, the fiery element in tremendous unrolling billows and masses of sheeted flame, enveloped the ... village. The frenzy of despair seized on all hearts, strong men bowed like reeds before the fiery blast, women and children, like frightened specters flitting through the awful gloom, were swept like autumn leaves. Crowds pushed for the bridge, but the bridge, like all else, was receiving its baptism of fire. Hundreds crowded into the river, cattle plunged in with them, and being huddled together in the general confusion of the moment, many who had taken to the water to avoid the flames were drowned. A great many were on the blazing bridge when it fell. The debris from the burning town was hurled over and on the heads of those who were in the water, killing many and maiming others so that they gave up to despair and sank to a watery grave."

Turning again, they struggled to reach the river itself, the banks of which by this time were beginning to fill up with refugees who had similar ideas. Father Pernin, still pushing his loaded handcart, soon found himself in the midst of this sea of humanity. He recalled, "The sawmill on the same side, at the angle of the bridge, as well as the large store belonging to the Company standing opposite across the road, were both on fire. The flames from these two edifices met across the road, and none could traverse this fiery passage without meeting with instant death. I was thus obliged to ascend the river on the left bank, above the dam, where the water gradually attained a great depth. After placing a certain distance between myself and the bridge, the fall of which I momentarily expected, I pushed my wagon as far into the water as possible. It was all that I could do. Henceforth I had to look to the saving of my life."

The only light available in the dark of the night was that given off by the fire itself, and that was hardly comforting, nor was it really illuminating, because by this time the air was so full of sand and ash that it created a fog that made the light turn back on itself, creating an eerie glow that seemed to taunt the dying and surviving alike like the open mouth of hell. For his part, Tisdale was not at all reluctant to choose water over fire. He continued his account: "I ran into the water, prostrated myself, and put my face in the water and threw water over my back and head. The heat was so intense that I could not keep my head out of the water for but a few seconds at a time, for the space of nearly an hour. Saw-logs in the river caught fire and burned in the water. A cow came to me, and rubbed her neck against me, and bawled most piteously. I heard men, women and children crying for help, but was utterly powerless to help anyone. What was my experience was the experience of others."

Chapter 6: Appalling Dangers

"It was about ten o'clock when we entered into the river. When doing so I neither knew the length of time we would be obliged to remain there, nor what would ultimately happen to us, yet, wonderful to relate my fate had never caused me a moment of anxiety from the time that, yielding to the involuntary impulse warning me to prepare for danger, I had resolved on directing my flight towards the river. Since then I had remained in the same careless frame of mind, which permitted me to struggle against the most insuperable obstacles, to brave the most appalling dangers, without ever seeming to remember that my life might pay the forfeit." - Reverend Peter Pernin, *The Great Peshtigo Fire: An Eyewitness Account*

It was clear that the only hope for salvation lay within the river itself, and yet people froze at the edge of the water, seemingly too overcome by shock or fear to actually plunge in. It was at this time that Father Pernin, accustomed to baptizing people to save their souls, found himself forcibly "baptizing" his neighbors to save them: "The whirlwind in its continual ascension had, so to speak, worked up the smoke, dust, and cinders, so that, at least, we could see clear before us. The banks of the river as far as the eye could reach were covered with people standing there, motionless as statues, some with eyes staring, upturned towards heaven, and tongues protruded. The greater number seemed to have no idea of taking any steps to procure their safety, imagining, as many afterwards acknowledged to me, that the end of the world had arrived and that there was nothing for them but silent submission to their fate. Without uttering a word ... I pushed the persons standing on each side of me into the water. One of these sprang back again with a half smothered cry, murmuring: "I am wet"; but immersion in water was better than immersion in fire. I caught him again and dragged him out with me into the river as far as possible. At the same moment I heard a splash of the water along the river's brink. All had followed my example. It was time; the air was no longer fit for inhalation, whilst the intensity of the heat was increasing. A few minutes more and no living thing could have resisted its fiery breath."

Tragically, it soon became obvious that even the water did not offer certain salvation from the fire. The wind continued to blow hot ash onto people as they stood in water up to their necks, forcing them to constantly wet their heads and faces. Women with long, thick hair soon learned that no matter how often they immersed themselves in the water, the fire would dry and ignite their hair almost as soon as their heads came out of the water. Father Pernin explained, "Once in water up to our necks, I thought we would, at least be safe from fire, but it was not so; the flames darted over the river as they did over land, the air was full of them, or rather the air itself was on fire. Our heads were in continual danger. It was only by throwing water constantly over them and our faces, and beating the river with our hands that we kept the flames at bay. Clothing and quilts had been thrown into the river, to save them, doubtless, and they were floating all around. I caught at some that came within reach and covered with them the heads of the persons who were leaning against or clinging to me. These wraps dried quickly in the furnace-like heat and caught fire whenever we ceased sprinkling them. The terrible whirlwind that had burst over us at the moment I was leaving home had, with its continually revolving circle of opposing winds, cleared the atmosphere. The river was as bright, brighter than by day, and the spectacle presented by these heads rising above the level of the water, some covered, some uncovered, the countless hands employed in beating the waves, was singular and painful in the extreme."

Other dangers lay in the chunks of burning wood that were regularly tossed into the river by the wind. If they landed on an uncovered head, they could render their victim unconscious or even kill them. At the very least, they would likely set someone's hair on fire. To protect themselves from this threat, some people tried holding a rescued pot or pan over their heads, but they quickly gave up on that idea when the handles became too hot to hold on to.

Of course, those in the river faced dangers besides those falling from the sky. For one thing, the river was full of burning logs and parts of nearby buildings that the wind had blown into the water. In addition to standing up to their necks in cold water and constantly dunking their heads or splashing water on themselves, those who survived that night also had to make sure that they dodged any fiery debris that came floating their way.

The people seeking safety in the river were not alone either, because many of the pets and livestock from the town also had made a run for the safety of the water and were now joining their masters in the fight for survival. This situation led to some very unique occurrences, such as this one described by Father Pernin: "Not far from me a woman was supporting herself in the water by means of a log. After a time a cow swam past. There were more than a dozen of these animals in the river, impelled thither by instinct, and they succeeded in saving their lives. The first mentioned one overturned in its passage the log to which the woman was clinging and she disappeared into the water. I thought her lost; but soon saw her emerge from it holding on with one hand to the horns of the cow, and throwing water on her head with the other. How long she remained in this critical position I know not, but I was told later that the animal had swam to shore, bearing her human burden safely with her; and what threatened to bring destruction to the woman had proved the means of her salvation."

Chapter 7: Nothing But Flames

"When turning my gaze from the river I chanced to look either to the right or left, before me or upwards, I saw nothing but flames; houses, trees, and the air itself were on fire. Above my head, as far as the eye could reach into space, alas! too brilliantly lighted, I saw nothing but immense volumes of flames covering the firmament, rolling one over the other with stormy violence as we see masses of clouds driven wildly hither and thither by the fierce power of the tempest. Near me, on the bank of the river, rose the store belonging to the factory, a large three-story building, filled with tubs, buckets, and other articles. Sometimes the thought crossed my mind that if the wind happened to change, we should be buried beneath the blazing ruins of this place, but still the supposition did not cause me much apprehension. When I was entering the water, this establishment was just taking fire; the work of destruction was speedy, for, in less than a quarter of an hour, the large beams were lying blazing on the ground, while the rest of the building was either burned or swept off into space." - Reverend Peter Pernin, *The Great Peshtigo Fire: An Eyewitness Account*

In addition to offering shelter from the fire, the river provided an excellent view of the fire as it burned on both sides. Tall buildings, once the pride of the town, burned that night like firewood carelessly tossed in a hot stove to make breakfast, and somewhat ironically, the buildings burned in the opposite order in which they had been built. First, the thin walls and siding were consumed, leaving behind a glowing skeleton that took a little longer to fall, as the boards used had been intended to stand for a hundred years. Then, with a great death cry, the skeleton itself burned away, sending the remaining boards crashing to the ground and transforming what had once been a shelter into a death trap.

Although it sounds odd, in addition to the many who burned to death that night or suffered some other death typical of being trapped in a fire, many lost their lives to the cold. It goes without saying that October is a cold month in Wisconsin, and the river to which many turned for safety spelled disaster because the water remained seasonally cold in spite of the flames overhead. Father Pernin explained, "Things went well enough with me during the first three or four hours of this prolonged bath, owing in part, I suppose, to my being continually in motion, either throwing water on my own head or on that of my neighbors. It was not so, however, with some of those who were standing near me, for their teeth were chattering and their limbs convulsively trembling. Reaction was setting in and the cold penetrating through their frames. Dreading that so long a sojourn in the water might be followed by severe cramps, perhaps death, I endeavored to ascend the bank a short distance, so as to ascertain the temperature, but my shoulders were scarcely out of the river, when a voice called to me: 'Father, beware, you are on fire!'"

The few who sought the warmth of the water closer to shore, where the fire heated the shallow depths, paid a high price, for the air there was filled with hot, poisonous gases that burned their lungs and their eyes. By 11:00 p.m., the entire village was on fire, and no one was able to make any effort to stop the conflagration. In fact, the heat was so high that the water in bottoms of deep wells boiled until they were dry, sometimes killing the people who had sought refuge in their once cool depths, while others who had hidden in root cellars and basements found themselves in red-hot ovens instead. Bodies in such places would not be found, replaced instead by skeletal remains curled in their final throes of agony. Some people were last seen diving into a damp, underground culver to escape the flames, but those looking for them later would find only a pile of ashes.

The wind soon turned on itself, creating that most dreaded of all natural occurrences – the fire tornado. As the fire cyclone danced through the town, it struck some buildings directly and ignited others just by being near them. Each building it consumed fed it with more energy until it towered into the sky. For the buildings and people not fortunate enough to be immediately consumed, the fire tornado picked them up, set them ablaze, and then spit them out again to launch a new conflagration far from its own immediate reach.

Many preachers in the churches surrounding Peshtigo had been preaching sermons predicting the end of the world over the long, dry summer, but for the one clergyman in the water that night, such predictions seemed unimportant compared to just surviving their peril one minute at a time. Father Pernin wrote:

> "The hour of deliverance from this prison of fire and water had not yet arrived-- the struggle was not yet over. A lady who had remained beside me since we had first taken to the river, and who, like all the others, had remained silent till then, now asked me:
>
> 'Father, do you not think this is the end of the world?'
>
> 'I do not think so,' was my reply, 'but if other countries are burned as ours seems to have been, the end of the world, at least for us, must be at hand.'
>
> After this both relapsed into silence."

As people pondered their fates and these kinds of questions, the fire around them had reached such an intensity that it actually set the soil ablaze. Part of the fuel for this endeavor came from the amount of sawdust that was mixed in with the dirt, which provided hot kindling. The other part consisted of the remains of roots and insects and their larvae. Those in the water watched in horror as the fire continued to burn across the shore on the river's edge and right up to the water itself. All the while, the sights above them were no better. Those who survived the dreadful night later spoke of how the sky itself appeared to be on fire. While this can be explained scientifically by the effect of a combination of the trees above them being in flames and the power of the reflective light bouncing off of the water, there's no doubt that part of their descriptions were generated by the sheer terror.

Chapter 8: An End to All Things

"There is an end to all things here below, even misfortune. The longed-for moment of our return to land was at length arriving, and already sprinkling of our heads was becoming unnecessary. I drew near the bank, seated myself on a log, being in this manner only partly immersed in the water. Here I was seized with a violent chill. A young man perceiving it threw a blanket over me which at once afforded me relief, and soon after I was able to leave this compulsory bath in which I had been plunged for about five hours and a half." - Reverend Peter Pernin, *The Great Peshtigo Fire: An Eyewitness Account*

While those in the water did not mention this phenomenon, many watching the fire burn from a safe distance outside of the town were able to record the dreadful sight. One man wrote, "Standing out on the Peshtigo road, we were a witness to the awful scene. The fire swept through the swamp and destroyed several out buildings in the rest of the Boom Co.'s place and Dr. Hall's together with a large barn containing nearly 100 tons of hay. The hay was the property of Mr. Bentley of Marinette. At this time the direction of the wind changed rapidly blowing from several points of the compass alternately. First from the south-west, then from the west, then from the north-west, then back again to the south, during which time we were visited by a series of whirlwinds which showered cinders and sparks in every conceivable direction. The fire having partly spent its fury here, cries of distress were heard down the river in the direction of the mouth. Steam whistles of the mills and tugs in the harbor blew the first alarm, and every man that could be spared went to the scene of disaster. From the rear of J. S. Dickey's store in the direction of the Bay all was one broad lurid sheet of flame as far as the eye could reach. At this time no hopes were entertained of saving anything. Men worked with the energy of despair."

Others recalled seeing what they described as "fire balloons," large black balls that seemed to float through the sky until they bumped into something, at which point they exploded and incinerated whatever they had touched. These balloons have never been completely explained by anyone, but many scientists believe that they were bubbles, perhaps created by superheated pine sap or perhaps filled with methane gas or some similarly flammable substance. While many people claimed they saw these balloons around Peshtigo that night, no one at any similar fire before or since has ever noticed such a phenomenon.

Then, suddenly, the firestorm was over. After having burned everything in its path to the river, it no longer had enough fuel to maintain itself. It was over as quickly as it had begun, though small fires continued to burn throughout the night. The fire burned on along the river across acres of forest all the way to the nearby town of Marinette, and in some places, the flames were so hot that ships in the nearby Green Bay had to fight off the effects of the heat and debris. Moreover, the smoke made it so dark during the next day that the lighthouse on Green Island in Green Bay stayed on, but one ship, the *George L. Newman*, was wrecked anyway. The smoke from the fire ultimately made it all the way to Ohio.

The lighthouse on Green Island

With the worst over, those who had remained in the water so long finally felt safe to emerge. Father Pernin later explained, "I CAME OUT of the river about half past three in the morning, and from that time I was in a very different condition, both morally and physically, to that in which I had previously been. Today, in recalling the past, I can see that the moment most fraught with danger was precisely that in which danger seemed at an end. The atmosphere, previously hot as the breath of a furnace, was gradually becoming colder and colder, and, after having been so long in the river, I was of course exceedingly susceptible to its chilly influence. My clothes were thoroughly saturated. There was no want of fire, and I easily dried my outer garments, but the inner ones were wet, and their searching dampness penetrated to my inmost frame, affecting my very lungs. Though close to a large fire, arising from heaps of burning fragments, I was still convulsively shivering, feeling at the same time a complete prostration of body and spirit. My chest was oppressed to suffocation, my throat swollen, and, in addition to an almost total inability to move, I could scarcely use my voice--utter even a word."

The survivors would soon be horrified to learn that more than 1,000 men, women, and children had died within a few hours that night, but as they began to crawl out of the water that night, they could only be concerned with their own immediate survival. The first thing they learned was that the ground, recently on fire, now provided soothing warmth to their freezing bodies. As Father Pernin put it, "Almost lifeless, I stretched myself out full length on the sand. The latter was still hot, and the warmth in some degree restored me. Removing shoes and socks I placed my feet in immediate contact with the heated ground, and felt additionally relieved." He continued, "I was lying beside the ruins of the large factory, the beams of which were still burning. Around me were piles of iron hoops belonging to the tubs and buckets lately destroyed. With the intention of employing these latter to dry my socks and shoes, now the only possessions left me, I touched them but found that they were still intolerably hot. Yet, strange to say, numbers of men were lying--some face downward--across these iron circles. Whether they were dead, or, rendered almost insensible from the effects of damp and cold, were seeking the warmth that the sand afforded me, I cannot say; I was suffering too intensely myself to attend to them. My eyes were now beginning to cause me the most acute pain, and this proved the case, to a greater or less extent, with all those who had not covered theirs during the long storm of fire through which we had passed. Notwithstanding I had kept head and face streaming with water, the heat had nevertheless injured my eyes greatly, though at the moment I was almost unconscious of the circumstance. The intense pain they now caused, joined to a feeling of utter exhaustion, kept me for a length of time extended on the earth."

Chapter 9: Survivors After a Battle

"Behold us then, all assembled in this valley like the survivors after a battle--some safe and well, others more or less wounded; some were very much so, especially a poor old woman who, fearing to enter the river completely, had lain crouched on the bank, partly in the water, partly out of it, and, consequently, exposed to the flames. She was now stretched on the grass, fearfully burned, and suffering intense agony, to judge from her heart-rending moans and cries. As she was dying, and had asked for me, I was brought to her, though I fear I proved but a poor consoler. I could not unclose my inflamed eyes, could scarcely speak, and felt so exhausted and depressed myself, that it was difficult to impart courage to others. The poor sufferer died shortly after." - Reverend Peter Pernin, *The Great Peshtigo Fire: An Eyewitness Account*

Those on the banks of the river in the early morning hours of October 9th soon realized that they were not yet out of danger. They were soaking wet and without shelter as the temperature dropped into the low 40s, and it soon became clear to everyone that the hypothermia they had avoided while in the water was still a significant threat. Father Pernin commented on the natural discomfort people commonly feel about undressing amid strangers and how it was brushed aside by many people that night: "When able, I dried my wet garments ... at the blazing ruins, and those near me did, the same. As each individual thought of himself, without minding his neighbor, the task was easy even to the most scrupulous and delicate. Putting on dry clothes afforded immediate relief to the pain and oppression of my chest, enabling me to breathe with more ease."

As they were finishing with such tasks, even those who had been nearly blinded by the fire began to notice that the sun was rising. Pernin noted, "Finally day dawned on a scene with whose horror and ruin none were as yet fully acquainted. I received a friendly summons to proceed to another spot where the greater number of those who had escaped were assembled, but the inflammation of my eyes had rapidly augmented, and I was now perfectly blind. Someone led me, however, to the place of refuge. It was a little valley near the river's edge, completely sheltered by sand hills, and proved to be the very place where I had intended taking refuge the evening previous, though prevented reaching it by the violence of the hurricane. Some had succeeded in attaining it, and had suffered comparatively far less than we had done. The tempest of fire had passed, as it were, above this spot, leaving untouched the shrubs and plants growing within it."

Of course, none were prepared for what they would see when the sun was fully up. The town they had called home was gone, as was the life they had known. A few days later, a reporter would speak with a local man who was there that morning: "From Mr. Place, who had just returned from the scene of the disaster, we learn that the town is destroyed, the Peshtigo Co.'s wooden ware factory, valued at several hundred thousand dollars; their water saw mill, grist mill, machine shop, sash factory, store and boarding house, ware houses — everything is gone. Stores, houses, churches, school houses, dwellings and everything was destroyed. The fire came upon them so suddenly that it was not in the reach of mortal power to stay its fury. [The] destruction of life was awful — awful to contemplate. Mr. Place informs us that he counted ten dead bodies in the streets as he passed. The loss of life at the present time is unknown, but it is estimated that over 100 have either perished or were rendered cripples for life. We have not yet been able to ascertain the names of the dead. One of the most terrible calamities that ever visited any country has befallen us. We know we can rely upon the sympathies of the good people outside, and if ever a case demand material aid prompt to allay some of the terrible suffering this is one."

Of course, those who had just barely survived the night had little time to think about their general surroundings, because many were more interested in finding missing loved ones or checking the status of abandoned homes and businesses. It would be easy to conclude that they should have known already who and what were lost, but hope always springs eternal during tragedies, a sentiment Father Pernin echoed in his account: "Those among us who had sufficient strength for the task dispersed in different directions to seek information concerning the friends whom they had not yet seen, and returned with appalling tidings relating to the general ruin and the number of deaths by fire. One of these told me that he had crossed to the other side of the river, and found all the houses as well as the church in ashes." With that news in hand, Pernin must have figured there was no reason for him to hurry home. Also, still nearly blinded from the fire, he probably doubted his ability to see what he was looking for, even if he found it intact. As a result, he did something else: "About eight o'clock, a large tent, brought on by the Company, was erected for the purpose of sheltering the women, children, and the sick. As soon as it was prepared someone came and urged me to profit of it. I complied, and stretched myself in a corner, taking up as little place as possible, so as to leave room for others. Ten o'clock arrived. After the sufferings of the night previous, many longed for a cup of hot tea or coffee, but such a luxury was entirely out of our reach, amid the desolation and ruin surrounding us. Some of the young men, after a close search, found and brought back a few cabbages from a neighboring field. The outer leaves, which were thoroughly scorched, were removed, and the inner part cut into thin slices and distributed among those capable of eating them. A morsel of cold raw cabbage was not likely to prove of much use in our then state of exhaustion, but we had nothing better at hand."

Chapter 10: Nothing Whatever Remained

A picture of one of the few pieces of lumber that survived the Peshtigo fire

"Of the houses, trees, fences that I had looked on three days ago nothing whatever remained, save a few blackened posts still standing.... The iron tracks of the railroad had been twisted and curved into all sorts of shapes, whilst the wood which had supported them no longer existed. The trunks of mighty trees had been reduced to mere cinders, the blackened hearts alone remaining. All around these trunks, I perceived a number of holes running downwards deep in the earth. They were the sockets where the roots had lately been. I plunged my cane into one of them, thinking what must the violence of that fire have been, which ravaged not only the surface of the earth, but penetrated so deeply into its bosom. Then I turned my wondering gaze in the direction where the town had lately stood, but nothing remained to point out its site except the boilers of the two locomotives, the iron of the wagon wheels, and the brick and stonework of the factory. ... Charred carcasses of horses, cows, oxen, and other animals lay scattered here and there. The bodies of the human victims--men, women, and children--had been already collected and decently interred--their number being easily ascertained by counting the rows of freshly-made graves." - Reverend Peter Pernin, *The Great Peshtigo Fire: An Eyewitness Account*

As bad as the situation around them was, the people of Peshtigo were soon encouraged by help from their neighbors. The people of nearby Marinette quickly heard about their tragedy and immediately dispatched helpful citizens who carried coffee, tea, and bread. As soon as the wagons bearing these people and supplies were emptied, the helpful neighbors loaded them with the most seriously injured and returned to Marinette with them. They continued their trips back and forth for many of the days that followed.

During the week immediately following the fire, there were many dead needing to be buried and barely enough men to do the job. Not surprisingly, many of the remains were burned beyond recognition and were consigned to mass graves, and other bodies were hardly more than bone and ash and could only be swept into large boxes. Father Pernin described the tragic attempts to lend some sort of dignity to many of the nearly 2,000 citizens who had perished: "I had not gone far before I saw much more than I would have desired to see. All in this line had perished, and perished in masses, for the vehicles were crowded with unfortunates who, flying from death, had met it all the sooner and in its most horrible form. In those places where the flames had enfolded their victims in their fiery clasp, nothing now was to be seen but calcined bones, charred mortal remains, and the iron circles of the wheels. It was with some difficulty that the human relics could be distinguished from those of the horses. The workmen of the Company were employed in collecting these sad memorials and burying them by the wayside, there to remain till such time as the friends of the dead might wish to reclaim and inter them in a more suitable manner."

The mass grave for victims of the Peshtigo fire

Of course, Father Pernin himself was in great demand, as those who were able to find the bodies of their loved ones wanted to see them decently buried. In the aftermath of the tragedy, the lines of religion and denomination quickly disappeared, and people who were lifelong Protestants were thankful to have their loved ones buried by a Catholic priest. Unfortunately, Pernin had nothing to offer them but himself and whatever part of the burial service he had memorized. He explained, "The graveyard lay close to the church, and I entered and waited there; for I expected momentarily the arrival of a funeral. It was that of a young man who had died the evening previous, in consequence of the terrible burns he had received. Never was burial service more poverty-stricken nor priest more utterly destitute of all things necessary for the performance of the sad ceremony. Nor church, nor house, nor surplice, stole nor breviary: nothing save prayer and a heartfelt benediction. I had felt this destitution still more keenly on two or three previous occasions when asked by the dying for the sacrament of Extreme Unction, which it was out of my power, alas, to administer to them. I left the graveyard with a heavy heart, and turned my steps in the direction of the river."

Among those who came to the town that week to help bury the dead was Mary Keith's father, who did not live in Peshtigo but had made many trips to the town to buy milk for his baby. Though his help was no doubt appreciated, people today might be more than a little uncomfortable with some of his interest in collecting souvenirs. Mary remembered, "My father helped pick up the dead and make rough boxes as there were not enough caskets. He put as many as five of a family in one casket as they were just bones. They found people who were not burned at all, just suffocated. Many saved themselves by going in the water with blankets wrapped around them, and some got down in wells and were saved that way. Chickens, sitting in their perches, were suffocated, not burned, and fish were on top of the water from the intense heat. Father said he found a young lady beside a log – she wasn't burned at all and had such a nice head of curly hair that he couldn't resist cutting a lock off. He always carried it in his purse and frequently showed it to us. My parents took a family of five who were burned and cared for them until they recovered."

Unfortunately, not everyone coming to Peshtigo during those first few terrible days were as helpful. Not even 24 hours had passed before Peshtigo came to face the same sort of shocking thefts that so often accompany any disaster. Father Pernin wrote of one such incident: "[A] man … had just been taken in the act of despoiling the bodies of the dead of whatever objects the fire had spared. A jury was formed, his punishment put to the vote, and he was unanimously condemned to be hanged on the spot. But where was a rope to be found? The fire had spared nothing. Somebody proposed substituting for the former an iron chain which had been employed for drawing logs, and one was accordingly brought and placed around the criminal's neck. Execution was difficult under the circumstances; and whilst the preparations dragged slowly on, the miserable man loudly implored mercy. The pity inspired by the mournful surroundings softened at length the hearts of the judges, and, after having made him crave pardon on his knees for the sacrilegious thefts of which he had been guilty, they allowed him to go free. It may have been that they merely intended frightening him."

The men's reaction to this sort of looting may have seemed too unduly harsh, but it's important to remember the incredibly dire circumstances under which the residents of Peshtigo were working. People had lost homes, families, and even animals. In fact, one of the most difficult things that many people faced, in addition to the obvious tragedy of lost human life, was the death of beloved pets. Father Pernin had freed his horse and tried to get his dog to follow him to the river in hopes of saving their lives, but it was ultimately for naught: "To find the streets was a difficult task, and it was not without considerable trouble that I succeeded at length in ascertaining the site where my house had lately stood. ... Here again was a total loss. A few calcined bricks, melted crystal ... alone pointed out where my house had once been, while the charred remains of my poor dog indicated the site of my bedroom. I followed then the road leading from my house to the river, and which was the one I had taken on the night of the catastrophe. There, the carcasses of animals were more numerous than elsewhere, especially in the neighborhood of the bridge. I saw the remains of my poor horse in the spot where I had last met him, but so disfigured by the fiery death through which he had passed that I had some difficulty in recognizing him. Those who have a horse, and appreciate the valuable services he renders them, will not feel surprised at my speaking twice of mine. There exists between the horse and his master a species of friendship akin to that which unites two friends, and which in the man frequently survives the death of his four-footed companion."

Chapter 11: Wandering Among the Ruins

The Peshtigo Fire Museum today

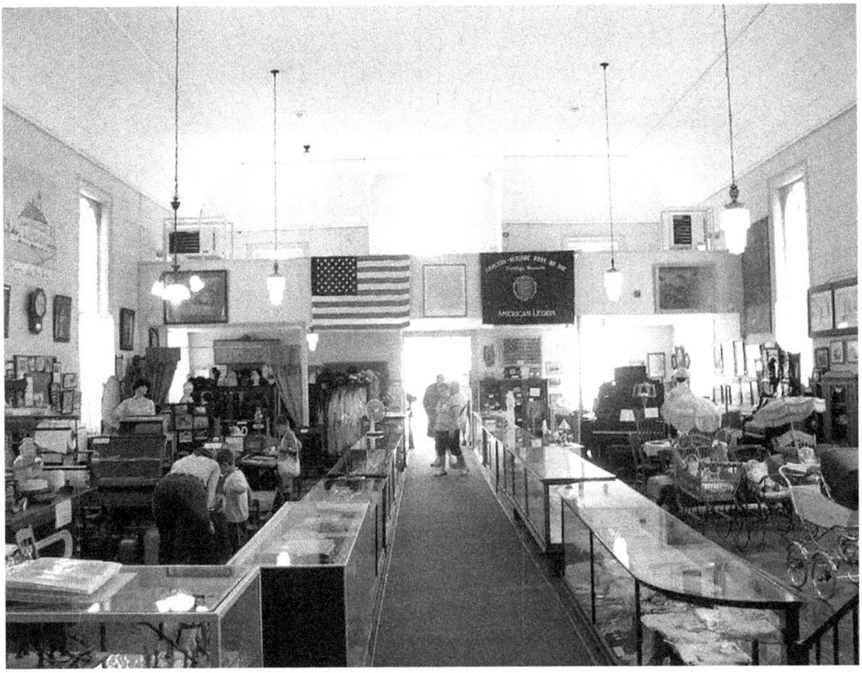
AMERICAN LEGION

Peshtigo artifacts now in the museum

"Whilst wandering among the ruins I met several persons, with some of whom I entered into conversation. One was a bereaved father seeking his missing children of whom he had as yet learned nothing. "If, at least," he said to me, with a look of indescribable anguish, "I could find their bones, but the wind has swept away whatever the fire spared." Children were seeking for their parents, brothers for their brothers, husbands for their wives…. The men I met, those sorrowful seekers for the dead, had all suffered more or less in the battle against wind and fire. Some had had a hand burned, others an arm or side; all were clothed in blackened, ragged garments, appearing, each one from his look of woeful sadness and miserable condition, like a ruin among ruins. They pointed out to me the places where they had found such and such individuals: there a mother lay prone on her face, pressing to her bosom the child she had vainly striven to save from the devouring element; here a whole family, father, mother, and children, lying together, blackened and mutilated by the fire fiend. Among the ruins of the boarding house belonging to the Company, more than seventy bodies were found, disfigured to such a fearful extent that it was impossible to tell either their age or sex. Farther on twenty more had been drawn from a well." - Reverend Peter Pernin, *The Great Peshtigo Fire: An Eyewitness Account*

In attempting to put together a list of those who died, even people trained to deal with such tragedies found themselves flummoxed. According to one report filed more than a year later, "Fully three months of hard and laborious work have been sent by Col. J.H. Leavenworth in making up a list of those burned; whole neighborhoods having been swept away without any warning, or leaving any trace, or record to tell the tale. It has been a difficult task to collect the number and names of families who have wholly or in part perished, although no pains have been spared to search out the survivors and make the records as nearly correct as possible. The list can be depended upon as far as it goes, but it is well known that the numbers of people were burned, particularly in the village of Peshtigo, whose names have never been ascertained, and probably never will be, as many of these were transient persons at work in the extensive manufactories, and all fled before the horrible tempest of fire, many of them caught in its terrible embrace with no record of their fate except their charred and blackened bones. The people of Peshtigo can all tell of acquaintances they had before the fire of whom they lost all knowledge since, and that many perished in the company's boarding house and the Catholic and Presbyterian churches, of whom not a vestige remains, there seems to be no reasonable doubt; for the very sands in the street were vitrified, and metals were melted in localities that seem impossible."

As soon as the dead were decently buried, the relatives remaining got busy writing letters to inform those living in other places about the tragedy that had struck their families. The people of Peshtigo in 1871 were living at the very height of the Victorian Era, a time when the niceties surrounding death and mourning had to be observed with the utmost care. Thus, as soon as she could access pen and paper, Martha Newberry Coon wrote to her sister-in-law, Mary Coon Powell: "I have bad news to tell. Charlie and his two little boys are gone. Oh! What a horrible death. There was a tornado of fire swept over the farming district and on the Peshtigo village, it came on us very suddenly; Charlie and his family started to flee. They got about a half mile from home when they went into a little pool of water, Charlie had the two children and some things he was trying to save. He passed through the water thinking to get farther away from the fire. Grace turned back into the water and was saved. In the water were brother William and his family; his wife and baby and his wife's sister; they were all that remained to tell the tale. Oh Mary, it was truly a night of horror, it rained fire; the air was on fire; some thought the last day had come, Mary -- my father, four brothers, two sisters-in-law and five of their children, two of Grace's, and three of brother Walter's, ah dear Mary, we are almost crazy, one can hardly keep one's senses together to write you anything."

Of course, the horror did not end with the fire. As Coon explained, there was also the difficulty of finding the bodies and just trying to figure out what to do next. Her letter soon took on the rambling tone of someone trying to write while still in shock: "George ... found Charlie and the children about five rods from where Grace was. ... poor old father, he was burned and most all of my brothers. ... Oh Mary, Grace has no clothes, I either, our eyes were all burned, but we are better now. Grace has poultices on her eyes, and they are getting better. George, Eddie and I were saved by fleeing to the river ... George and I did not save any clothes. Eddie was in bed, I got him up and dressed him, without his stockings. He is without a stocking to his name. It seems that I did not want anything more ... George found the bodies of all our folks except three, father, one brother and his wife. He is going tomorrow with some men, and some boards to bury them. One brother was all burned except for his face. Oh it is too horrible to write about or to believe ... Those who never prayed before prayed that night."

There were many in shock that day, but as with so many other disasters, the survivors of this one rallied and began to make plans to rebuild their home and their towns. In fact, rather than dying away, Peshtigo experienced something of a renaissance in the year that followed the fire. As new buildings grew up around the town, the population skyrocketed as men and their families moved in to help rebuild the town. The Peshtigo fire of 1871 was the deadliest fire in American history, and it scorched an area twice the size of Rhode Island, but Peshtigo's current population is higher than ever before.

Bibliography

Ball, Jacqueline A. *Wildfire! The 1871 Peshtigo Firestorm*. New York: Bearport Pub., 2005.

Bergstrom, Bill. *Peshtigo*. Philadelphia: Xlibris, 2003.

Pernin, Peter. "The Great Peshtigo Fire: An Eyewitness Account," *Wisconsin Magazine of History*, 54: 4 (Summer, 1971), 246-272.

Wells, Robert W. *Fire at Peshtigo*. Englewood Cliffs, NJ: Prentice-Hall, 1968.

CPSIA information can be obtained
at www.ICGtesting.com
Printed in the USA
LVHW041720260919
632370LV00010B/817/P